T0311707

Cambridge Elements ≡

Elements in Earth System Governance
edited by
Frank Biermann
Utrecht University
Aarti Gupta
Wageningen University
Michael Mason
London School of Economics and Political Science (LSE)

JUST TRANSITIONS

Promise and Contestation

Dimitris Stevis
Colorado State University

CAMBRIDGE
UNIVERSITY PRESS

Shaftesbury Road, Cambridge CB2 8EA, United Kingdom

One Liberty Plaza, 20th Floor, New York, NY 10006, USA

477 Williamstown Road, Port Melbourne, VIC 3207, Australia

314–321, 3rd Floor, Plot 3, Splendor Forum, Jasola District Centre, New Delhi – 110025, India

103 Penang Road, #05–06/07, Visioncrest Commercial, Singapore 238467

Cambridge University Press is part of Cambridge University Press & Assessment, a department of the University of Cambridge.

We share the University's mission to contribute to society through the pursuit of education, learning and research at the highest international levels of excellence.

www.cambridge.org
Information on this title: www.cambridge.org/9781108947008

DOI: 10.1017/9781108936569

First published 2023

A catalogue record for this publication is available from the British Library.

ISBN 978-1-108-94700-8 Paperback
ISSN 2631-7818 (online)
ISSN 2631-780X (print)

Just Transitions

Promise and Contestation

Elements in Earth System Governance

DOI: 10.1017/9781108936569
First published online: April 2023

Dimitris Stevis
Colorado State University

Author for correspondence: Dimitris Stevis, dimitris.stevis@colostate.edu

Abstract: Just transition prompts us to explore a number of important dimensions of earth system governance research, including sustainability transformations, inequality, power and justice. This Element aims to place just transition in the dynamics of the world political economy over the last several decades and to offer an overview of the varieties of just transitions based on an analytical scheme that focuses on their breadth (coverage), depth (social and ecological priorities) and ambition. The focus on breadth, depth and ambition centres on power, inequality and injustice and allows us to analyze and compare just transitions as a prerequisite for their fuller interpretation.

Keywords: just transition, environmental justice, social justice, ecosocial governance, ecosocial politics

ISBNs: 9781108947008 (PB), 9781108936569 (OC)
ISSNs: 2631-7818 (online), 2631-780X (print)

Contents

1 Introduction

From its origins in a small US labour union that no longer exists, the explicit concept and strategy of just transition is now on the agenda, if not the practice, of intergovernmental organizations and negotiations, governments, environmentalists, business, churches and labour unions around the world (JTRC 2018; Morena, Krause and Stevis 2020; WRI 2022). In general terms, it calls for treating workers and communities affected by transitions in a humane and just way. In its most prominent version, it calls for just environmental transitions, particularly energy ones. Sustainable development also foregrounds a synthesis of the ecological (sustainability) and the social (development). However, just transition centres justice – and thus (in)equality and power – and envisions abandoning, rather than modifying, ecologically harmful practices.

Accordingly, just transition prompts us to explore a number of important dimensions of earth system governance research, including sustainability transformations, inequality, power, democracy and justice (e.g., Burch et al. 2019; Biermann and Kalfagianni 2020; Pickering et al. 2022). My primary goals in this Element are: (1) to place explicit just transitions, that is proposals and policies that employ the term, in the dynamics of the world political economy over the last several decades and, in particular, the politics for a more egalitarian social (and now ecosocial[1]) society; and (2) to offer an overview of the varieties of explicit just transitions based on an analytical scheme that focuses on their breadth (coverage), depth (social and ecological priorities) and ambition. I believe that placing just transitions in their historical dynamics can shed light on our contemporary understandings and uses of the strategy. The focus on breadth, depth and ambition foregrounds power, inequality and injustice and allows us to interpret and compare just transitions as a prerequisite for their fuller understanding. The politics of policy formation and implementation are also discussed as necessary but they are not the central focus here.

There are four additional and related reasons why the study of just transition is useful (see Räthzel and Uzzell 2013; Hampton 2015; Räthzel, Stevis and Uzzell 2018, 2021; Bell 2020). Most immediately it challenges the view that labour unions are uniformly opposed to environmentalism and opens up a rich area of research and practice that has only recently received attention. Second, it invites us to examine the centrality of people as workers if we are to advance a just and ecological future. The vast majority of people, regardless of ideology, gender, ethnicity, sexuality or other characteristics are waged or unwaged

---

[1] I will be using 'ecosocial', which is becoming more common in labour environmentalism, but one could very well use 'socioecological'.

workers. Acccess inequalities are largely due to people not being able or allowed to work or not being properly compensated for working. Addressing the impact of transitions on people as workers closes a major gap in our understanding of social and environmental politics and policy. This brings us closer to the third reason – work (Bottazzi 2019; Räthzel and Uzzell 2019; Iskander and Lowe 2020; ILO 2022; OECD 2022; World Economic Forum 2022) Whether we work, how we work, what we produce and why we produce it, are at the heart of political economy and ecology. The production process is the terrain in which power relations among workers, managers, capitalists, communities and states play out with profound implications for the organization of the political economy. What we produce determines what we consume, more so than the other way around. Why we produce something forces us to think about its uses. Can a production process or a product be considered 'green', for instance, if its purpose is war (Sommer 2022)? In my view, workers and work provide the lenses through which we can explore transitions that include all affected without 'all' becoming an empty signifier. Finally, the study of explicit just transitions forces us to explore the politics over preserving and expanding egalitarian ecosocial policies (whether social liberal, socialdemocratic or demo-cratic socialist) under conditions of global neoliberalism in its cosmopolitan, nationalist or nativist versions (for some historical background see Mazower 2013). The thrust of this Element, in fact, is that just transitions are best understood as part of the longer and broader politics over ecosocial policies rather than transitions or transformations in some ahistorical sense.

Clarifications and Evidence

Four clarifications are necessary at this point. First, what qualifies as transition in just transition? I take up the topic in more detail in Section 4, but here I would suggest that most people researching and working on just transition refer to an irrevocable change due to profound socio-technical shifts, such as the various industrial revolutions in modern times, sometimes associated with or driven by policies, such as decarbonization policies. These transitions involve major changes in what is produced, how and where and, thus, by whom. Often workers cannot find work elsewhere since the whole sector, including their skills, disappears. However, as I discuss in Section 4, I also think that transitions are due to additional shifts in the political economy, whether relocation or changes in the nature of the product, such as electric vehicles, in an otherwise thriving sector. They are also driven by social emancipations and demographic changes that bring new people, hitherto excluded, into the waged labour force. Finally, I believe that any transition, such as the closing of an automobile plant or a supermarket or a school qualifies as a transition in need of a just transition. In short, I do not believe that the transitions in 'just transitions' should be limited to macrohistorical or macroeconomic transitions. My approach makes transitions, and just transitions, central to the organization of the political economy in the same way that would be the case with other public goods. For example, socialized healthcare does not kick in only when there is a major transition in health – whether due to a pandemic or a medical breakthrough. Rather, it is an integral element of the social welfare political economy, in its various permutations. As I will argue, the strategy of just transition was and is an integral part of the broader politics over ecosocial welfare, broadly construed.

This is so because just transition is a contested concept politically and conceptually – the second clarification. Politically not everyone involved or affected by transitions supports just transitions even if they support other social or environmental welfare policies (e.g., United Mine Workers of America 2021). Many unions, communities, corporations and states are indifferent or opposed to transitions. Others accept the unavoidability of transitions but prefer economic development policies in which justice is an afterthought. Finally, some of the existing just transition policies and proposals are arguably less egalitarian or inclusive than the more inclusive economic development policies.

Quite often analysts argue that unless we agree on its definition and operationalization, a concept is useless analytically and practically. I believe that such an approach would render much of the social sciences, and beyond, incapacitated. The debates over the origins and future of international relations, as a discipline, suggest that hegemonic definitions and operationalizations are not independent of hegemonic institutional arrangements (e.g., Weaver and Tickner 2009; Hagmann and Biersteker 2014). As Connelly (2007) has argued, this is not a reason to reject a concept. Rather, it calls for analysts to reflect on how social actors, including the analysts themselves, delineate and operationalize a concept and what worldview is reflected by that (Biermann and Kalfagianni 2020). This allows us to have a more productive, if not easy, discussion about how and why we use concepts in particular ways – rather than treating operationalization as a technical and only process (Lohmann 2009; Aradau and Huysmans 2013; Seabrooke and Wigan 2015).

Third, and following Hopwood, Mellor and O'Brien (2005) I differentiate ecosocial policies, including just transitions, in terms of their focus on (in) equality and standing for nature, ranging from those that privilege social inequality and anthropocentrism to those that move us in the direction of a socially and ecologically egalitarian society. I add to that scheme the need to examine even the most egalitarian ecosocial policies within their broader spatial, temporal and social contexts. This is not an argument of moving from problems and contestations to a world in which difference and disagreement disappear. Rather, my argument is that different political economies/ecologies provide different parameters within which people deliberate and contest priorities (Cox 1981; Wright 2013; Marchese 2022).[2] In a palpable way, one can see the difference in comparing health care debates in countries with and without socialized healthcare or with and without women's rights.

Finally, the information I use is based on the historical record and on contemporary practice and debates. The historical record includes primary and secondary sources as well as interviews with labour environmentalists that were and are involved in the politics of just transition (e.g., Stevis 2021c). I have followed contemporary practice and debates through secondary and primary sources, interviews and engaged research and practice networks, particularly as part of the JTRC, the Just Transition Listening Project (JTLP 2021) and the ongoing Just Transition and Care Initiative. At the global level, I have followed more closely the just transition politics of global unions (e.g., Stevis and Felli 2015; Stevis 2021a) and, increasingly other social movements. At the national level I have paid close attention to just transition debates in the USA (Stevis 2018), Canada, Greece and the EU. At the sub-national level I have followed closely the just transition policies of the State of Colorado and the City of Longmont (also in Colorado) as well as local transitional policies in the USA (JTLP 2021). Moreover, my research on just transitions has reached beyond energy and climate (e.g., Stevis, Krause and Morena 2021).

Outline

In Sections 2 and 3, I place the trajectory of explicit just transitions within the longer history over social and, more recently, ecosocial politics. Section 2 covers the period from the 1960s to 2001 as the decline of the post–Second World War embedded liberalism, in a liberal capitalist country with limited social welfare policies to begin with, led to the rise and decline of explicit just transition in the USA. I point out here that the major views for and against just transition were evident by the end of this period. In Section 3, I discuss how a network of national and global labour environmentalists placed just transition on the global agenda, increasingly as a strategic intervention in global climate politics. In addition to grounding just transition historically, these sections also anticipate the variability of just transition in terms of breadth, depth and ambition.

---

[2] In his interview with Marchese, Herman Daly, not an egalitarian, argues that 'in order to move from our present growth economy to a steady-state economy, that's going to imply some important design principles – some changes in the fundamental design'.

This analytical scheme, which owes a great deal to my collaboration with Romain Felli (Stevis and Felli 2016) and the JTRC (2018),[3] is developed and employed in Sections 4, 5 and 6, where I illustrate its main components using just transition policies and well-developed policy proposals from around the world and across sectors. What I hope becomes apparent is that the analytical scheme can be employed to explore other important concepts, whether justice, democracy or power.

In Section 4, I explore the scale and scope of just transitions (breadth). Does a just transition proposal or policy cover the whole geographic and temporal scale of a transition or only parts of it?[4] Does its scope cover all sectors and affected people and nature or only some? Is there an alignment between scale and scope? Is there an alignment between the scales and scopes of the transition and the transition policy or are they at odds with each other? And, if so, is the just transition policy supported by adequate and appropriate resources or is it largely performative? What are the overall patterns in terms of the breadth of just transitions currently?

In Section 5, I turn to the purpose of just transitions (their depth) by focusing on social and ecological equality and justice. The social goals of a transitional policy may be more or less egalitarian and thus just or unjust. However, social equality and justice can take place at the expense of nature, as much as environmental quality can be enhanced at the expense of social equality (Hopwood, Mellor and O'Brien 2005). Is there an alignment between social and ecological priorities? And, as with breadth, is the just transition policy supported by adequate and appropriate resources or is it largely performative? What are the overall patterns in terms of the depth of just transitions?

Section 6 focuses on the ambition of just transitions. In the first part I argue that the ambition of just transitions, or any other policies, must consider both their depth and their breadth. Labelling policies that are limited to particular places and people as transformative reinforces the differentiation between insiders and outsiders that is central to domestic and international political theory and practice. With that in mind, I contrast just transitions in terms of the ecosocial political economy/ecology that they are likely to advance. In the conclusion, I comment on the need to pay attention to both the form and purpose of just transitions and reflect on the main themes explored in this Element.

---

[3] Rebecca Shelton – now Director of Policy at the Appalachian Citizens' Law Center – played a key role in the development of the JTRC's analytical scheme.

[4] Of course, we should also ask whether the transition itself rises up to the challenge at hand.

2 Just Transition as a Response to Neoliberalism in the USA: 1970s to 2001

A few years ago I interviewed a unionist, with a doctorate in philosophy, who had played a central role in promoting labour environmentalism and just transition in the Canadian labour movement. Before I could ask my first question, he informed me that we would not go any further unless it was clear to me that just transition was a response to the decline of the already modest social welfare state in the USA and Canada, as a result of the resurgence of neoliberal globalization since the 1970s. This interpretation has been reinforced by subsequent research and confirmed by others involved in the development and uses of the strategy from the 1970s to the present. In fact, the rise of neoliberalism, and efforts to contain and re-regulate it, also permeate industrial relations and environmentalism. For my purposes, therefore, the historicization and politicization of just transition is relational (Stevis and Assetto 2001) and embedded within the broader dynamics of the world political economy.

In its simplest form, the historicization (Gismondi 2019) of just transition traces its trajectory and the views of the actors involved. It is useful to know that this is a strategy developed by unions – challenging the myth that unions and environmentalism do not mix – and that it was never intended to only cover energy. And it is also important to know that many unions were and remain resolutely against the strategy, and that labour environmentalism is one broad and diverse tendency within the labour movement (Barca 2012; Räthzel and Uzzell 2012, 2013). However, historicization requires that we also politicize a practice or proposal by placing it within the political economy in which it has emerged and has been deployed over the years (Healy and Barry 2017; for a somewhat different approach, see Jenkins et al. 2020). Just transition policies in a liberal capitalist society, like the USA, are not the same as those in a coordinated capitalist society, like Sweden, in which many of the social welfare demands of explicit just transition are already policy, what may be called implicit or embedded just transition (Krause et al. 2022).

Explicit Just Transition as a Response to Neoliberalism in the USA

Neoliberalism

After the First World War, the state played a dominant role in world politics, largely in the Global North, but also in Latin America and parts of Asia, in response to geopolitical conflicts, the interwar social revolutions and the Great Depression. As Karl Polanyi argued, society responded to the ravages of the market through another Great Transformation (Polanyi 1944). The 'embedded liberalism' of the post–Second World War years was intended to prevent a repetition of the social disruptions of the interwar era and to contain communism (Ruggie 1982). During that period, capitalism was rebuilt by accommodating workers and families through more or less ambitious social reforms, the main goal of which was to prevent even more ambitious policies (Esping-Andersen 1990; Hall and Sockice 2001; Frieden 2020). Analysts of varieties of capitalism and the social welfare state differentiate between liberal capitalism in countries such as the USA, the UK or Australia, characterized by narrow versions of industrial relations and weaker social welfare policies, and coordinated capitalism in Western and Northern European countries, characterized by more institutionalized industrial relations and stronger social welfare policies. Over time, research on capitalism, business systems and the social welfare state has expanded this categorization (Gould et al. 2015; Witt et al. 2018; Mandelli 2022).

The unravelling of this compromise started during the early 1960s with the promotion of trade liberalization, and was at full steam by the mid-1970s, beginning with the USA. In the decades that followed, neoliberalism spread throughout the rest of the industrial world (Mazower 2013; Frieden 2020) and was imposed on the Global South, which had promoted the more statist New International Economic Order during the 1960s and 1970s. The challenges that major industrializing countries are now posing are arguably within the parameters of capitalism and, in fact, strengthen capitalism (Stephen 2014; Nayyar 2016; Brand and Wissen 2021). The most important current tension is not that of capitalism versus socialism but that of nativist versus cosmopolitan capitalism (Bhambra, Medien and Tilley 2020), combined with hegemonic competition. This 'nationalization within the world economy', in the words of Nikolai Bukharin (1973 [1915]), is as incendiary now as it was just before the First World War, at the end of another period of neoliberal globalization.

Rather than social re-regulation, corporate social responsibility, increasingly buttressed by multi-stakeholderism (Transnational Institute 2019) is exerting significant attraction not only on societal forces that would prefer socially unregulated markets but also on many that are critical of them. National and global unions have sought to tame and redirect corporate social responsibility, but the results are episodic and do not indicate a change in power relations between capital and labour. For a significant portion of civil society, corporate social responsibility has become the systemic alternative to neoliberalism, contributing to capitalism's hegemony (Shamir 2010, 2011; Mousu 2020) rather than its re-embedding (Ruggie 2018).

But it was not just the overall political economy and industrial relations that became more neoliberal since the 1970s. Environmentalism did too. Environmentalism has always been diverse, with social and liberal worldviews competing for primacy from the very beginning of modern environmentalism (Stevis 2010b). By the 1990s, liberal environmentalism had emerged hegemonic in policy if not in theory, as evident by climate negotiations, among other (Bernstein 2001; Stevis and Assetto 2001; Felli 2021).

Liberal environmentalism's ascent was not easy, any more than the rise of liberal feminism or unionism has been. While greenwashing is common, liberal environmentalism reflects a genuine commitment to a particular political ecology that reinforces capitalism as it expands it into nature (for older and more recent statements, see Lovins 1975; Barbier 2022). The deep competition between the fossil fuel and renewable energy sectors of capital is evidence of real differences between liberal environmentalists and liberal anti-environmentalists over change within, rather than of, capitalism (Ougaard 2016). The decline of embedded liberalism, along with the rise of corporate social responsibility and liberal environmentalism, provide the political contexts within which the history of labour environmentalism and just transition unfolded.

Labour environmentalism refers to the views of unions and workers towards the environment (for historical overviews, see Silverman 2004, 2006; Barca 2012) and has diverse roots that are much broader than just transition. Some labour environmentalists, in fact, are opposed or sceptical of just transition. And, as mentioned in Section 1, many unions do not have an environmental policy or are opposed to labour environmentalism. In what follows I provide some examples of labour environmentalism to highlight its breadth, even during the 1960s and 1970s. It is much richer and more diverse now (Räthzel and Uzzell 2013; Räthzel, Stevis and Uzzell 2018, 2021).

Labour Environmentalism without Job Blackmail

During the early 1970s, Australian unions came out against a uranium mine and, more significantly, against building in natural areas. The New South Wales Builders Labourers' Federation did not simply oppose new construction but actually called upon its members to refuse to work on such projects. In short, the union challenged developers over what ought to be built, and where, rather than how it ought to be built (Burgmann and Burgmann 1998).

In 1973, IG Metall, the largest manufacturing union in Germany, then and now, organized its only special conference on quality of life, inspired by the debates around the environment emerging from the Club of Rome and the Stockholm Conference (see Siegmann 1985: 12–20 and throughout). The nature of work and quality of life were central to the conference, as they were central to IG Metall. This, then, was an approach that sought to reconcile work and the environment, presaging the strategy of ecological modernization.

Another iconic example of labour environmentalism took place in the UK from the mid 1970s to the early 1980s in response to the shuttering of the Lucas combine – a manufacturer of military equipment (Räthzel, Uzzell and Elliott 2010; Cooley 2016).[5] Rather than accept that decision passively, blue- and white-collar workers – through a deliberate and challenging process – pooled their skills to propose alternative products that were socially and environmentally positive and innovative. The Lucas Plan was not effective because of corporate and state opposition, but it has left behind the vision of workers as active participants in shaping a transition.

It is tempting to conclude that labour environmentalism is a product of the North, but that is not the case. Liberation theology influenced some Latin American social activists during the 1960s and 1970s, including in the direction of considering the interface between social and environmental priorities (Barca 2012; Barca and Milanez 2021; Leandro, Tropia and Räthzel 2021). One example of that was the Rubber Tappers' Union organized in Brazil in 1975. In the view of seasoned analysts, this more inclusive ecosocial approach continues to influence Latin American labour environmentalism and is reflected in the Development Platform of the Americas, launched by the Trade Union Confederation of the Americas (TUCA) in 2014 and revised in 2020 (TUCA 2020).

These examples serve to show that labour environmentalism is much broader than just transitions. This is also evident in the USA, where the explicit just transition narrative emerged (on the history of labour environmentalism in the USA, see Siegmann 1985; Gordon 2004; Dewey 2019). During the 1940s, a logging union proposed a far-reaching conservation plan that would mitigate employment and resource fluctuations in the Western USA and Canada (Loomis 2021). In 1965, the United Automobile Workers (UAW) organized the first and largest conference on clean water, alarmed over the impacts of cities and manufacturing on the Great Lakes – one of the largest sources of fresh water in the world. This and other initiatives were motivated by the union's long-standing view of itself as an organization representing workers and society at large. Reflecting this commitment, the UAW, as well as other unions, also played a key role in supporting the first Earth Day in 1970.

Labour Environmentalism with Job Blackmail

The 1960s and early 1970s were one of the most critical periods in US history. The Great Society programmes adopted during the Johnson Presidency (1963–8) are considered, along with the New Deal of the 1930s, as the major pillars of the

---

[5] This example could be placed under labour environmentalism and job blackmail. However, I am placing it here because it reflects an attempt to bypass the power of capital.

US social welfare society. The mobilizations of the period forced the Nixon administration to adopt some of the strongest environmental policies in US history on clean air, water, endangered species and, to a lesser degree, occupational health and safety. While the Nixon administration was forced to adopt these policies, it, along with business, saw them as a frontal attack on capitalism, as exemplified by the Powell Memorandum of 1971.[6] During that same time, the Southern States in the USA intensified their anti-union policies to attract business, first from elsewhere in the USA and then, increasingly, from Europe and Japan (Cobb and Stueck 2005). The oil crisis of 1973 signalled a formal end to the post-war settlement in the USA, with other industrial countries following during the subsequent two decades.

In a 1972 presentation to a conference on jobs and the environment, Leonard Woodcock, the president of the UAW, reasserted the union's commitment to environmental policies and highlighted the Nixon administration's efforts, in collaboration with capital, to develop a 'job blackmail' strategy: blaming environmental or any other social regulatory laws for the closing and relocation of a facility (Woodcock 1972; Kazis and Grossman 1991[1982]). Woodcock realized that collective bargaining – even for a powerful union such as the UAW – could not prevent corporate automation and relocation. He called for policies that gave workers, unions and communities the legal right to pre-emptively challenge corporate decisions, and eased the impacts of transitions on workers and communities – what today we call 'just transition'. However, the capacity of the UAW and other manufacturing unions to exert influence over core management decisions had been given away by the UAW itself with the 1950 'Treaty of Detroit' (Loomis 2018). That agreement between UAW and General Motors initiated a pattern whereby unions could negotiate wages, pensions and health benefits that were now fully associated with the company – thus privatizing social welfare. In exchange, management obtained the right to decide on location, production and automation, among other things. While many collective agreements, particularly in manufacturing, included provisions covering workers during transitional periods, these became less and less consequential as business started relocating and automating, and unions lost members.

During the 1970s, capital and anti-environmentalist unions were successful in framing environmental policies in terms of 'jobs versus environment', rendering the environment heteronomous. Labour environmentalists, including the Oil, Chemical and Atomic Workers' Union (OCAW), proposed 'just

---

[6] Lewis Powell Jr was a business lawyer at the time. Nixon nominated him to the Supreme Court soon thereafter. See www.google.com/search?client=safari&rls=en&q=Lewis+Powell+memorandum&ie=UTF-8&oe=UTF-8.

transition' (the term was not used until 1995) to blunt this framing, in the process adding to its discursive hegemony. An alternative framing argued for 'jobs and environment' (Grossman and Daneker 1979). In aggregate terms, environmental policies created and continue to create jobs in remediation and in new industries, while most job losses were, and are, due to automation, liberalized trade, the reorganization of supply chains and weak unions, rather than environmental policies. However, environmental transitions, like all transitions, do generate conjunctural and longer-term shifts that affect particular workers and communities. Hence, there was and remains a real tension between those who see just transition as a necessary component of green transitions and those who place their hopes in green industrial policy (Stevis 2021c).

I argue here that the 'jobs versus environment' and 'jobs and environment' binary has been and can be modified to include 'jobs *versus* environment with and without just transition' and 'jobs *and* environment with and without just transition'. In fact, the original OCAW proposal was one of 'jobs and environment with just transition' even though it was, unfortunately, framed as 'jobs versus environment' (see Figure 1). An example of the first category would be the attitude of many fossil fuel unions, who are opposed to just transition because they are opposed to the decarbonization transition. Some manufacturing and construction unions, on the other hand, prefer to advocate for green industrial transitions that are likely to benefit them, while creating alliances with capital. An example of that in the USA would be the BlueGreen Alliance (BGA) of unions and environmentalists (BGA 2022). The 'jobs versus environment with just transition' approach is less prominent if we accept my argument that the strategy of the OCAW was, in substance, one of 'jobs and environment with

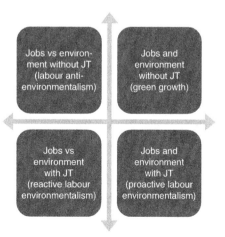

Figure 1 Configurations of jobs, environment and just transitions

just transition' (in fact, see Public Health and Labor Institutes 2000). However, quite likely, some unions, corporations and governments are employing the 'jobs versus environment with just transition' narrative to delay both green and just transitions. Finally, the 'jobs and environment with just transition' approach, which is the subject of this Element, is broad enough to include transformative initiatives like the Lucas Plan and neoliberal approaches like that of The B Team business coalition (Just Transition Centre and The B Team 2018).

The Rise of Explicit Just Transition in North America: 1970s to 2001

Labour environmentalism grew significantly in the USA during the 1970s, with a number of unions playing an important role, including the International Woodworkers, the United Steelworkers (USW) and the OCAW. In fact, labour environmentalists, including from within the UAW, along with African American unionists and environmental and urban community activists, organized a conference on economic and environmental justice in 1976 (Gordon 2004; Rector 2014). However, by the end of the decade, the UAW had moved away from its environmentalism, falling victim to job blackmail. Collaboration and debates between unions and environmentalists continued into the 1980s, in the face of the Reagan administration and strong resistance from fossil fuel unions and conservative building and construction unions (Gordon 2004; Dewey 2019; interviews).

It is within that broader context that Tony Mazzocchi – a trade unionist working on occupational safety and health policy for OCAW – played a central role (Leopold 2007). As far back as the 1950s, Mazzocchi had been exposed to social environmentalist ideas associated with Barry Commoner (1972). Unlike many fellow trade unionists, his priority was not to preserve all jobs. He acknowledged that certain jobs were too detrimental to workers, society and the environment, and should therefore be scrapped or replaced by automation. In all cases, the priority should be to empower workers and communities, and enable them 'to know and act', especially in the face of job blackmail (Kazis and Grossman 1991 [1982]). This, he believed, could be achieved through the strengthening of the social welfare state.

During the 1970s, he and others evoked the GI Bill, which was intended to help integrate soldiers, largely white males, back into society after the Second World War, as an example of a policy that could be applied to sunsetting industries, particularly those that were environmentally damaging. During the late 1970s, the International Woodworkers of America supported the expansion of the Redwoods National Park, at great cost to its left-leaning leadership (JTLP 2021). Agreed upon in 1978 between unions, environmentalists and policy makers, the policy provided for the kinds of transitional policies eventually associated with just transition. It was only after that union broke up into Canadian and US unions[7] that the latter adopted the 'jobs versus environment' narrative, leading to the conflict between ecosystem protection and unregulated logging (the 'spotted owl' conflict; Loomis 2021).

Mazzocchi and the OCAW framed just transition as a solution to the 'jobs versus environment' dilemma and both he and the OCAW considered just transition as one element of a stronger social and environmental welfare state. This was reflected in the programme adopted at the 1988 OCAW Convention, reiterated in a resolution passed at the 1991 Convention calling for 'a new social, political, and economic agenda', which set goals for the 1990s, including national health care, a Labor Party alternative, environmental protection, a Superfund for Workers, and international trade unionism (interviews with principal participants; see also OCAW 1991; Wykle et al. 1991; Mazzocchi 1993; Hampton 2015).

The Superfund for Workers evoked the federal Superfund policy that was adopted in 1980 to clean up thousands of contaminated industrial sites. It was in 1995 that the term 'just transition' was first used by representatives of the OCAW and the Communications, Energy and Paperworkers Union of Canada (CEP) that included the erstwhile Canadian part of the OCAW, at a presentation to the International Joint Commission on Great Lakes Water Quality.

> We propose that a special fund be established; a just-transition fund which we've called in the past a superfund for workers. Essentially this fund will provide the following: full wages and benefits until the worker retires or until he or she finds a comparable job; two – up to four years of tuition stipends to attend vocational schools or colleges plus full income while in school; three – post-educational stipends or subsidies if no jobs at comparable wages are available after graduation; and four – relocation assistance. (Leopold 1995: 83)

Even as a stand-alone policy this would have been a major expansion of social welfare in the USA and most other countries. However, as noted, the OCAW placed just transition within a broader agenda that included green industrial policy. Moreover, just transition was part of the even broader platform of the Labor Party that the OCAW tried to create throughout the 1990s. The party's 1996 platform called for an end to bigotry, universal health care and education, family and community time through the reduction of working time, the regulation of corporations and the reduction of their power, and worker participation in the design and organization of work (Labor Party 1996).

---

[7] During the late 1970s and early 1980s, some binational unions, including the OCAW, broke up into their US and Canadian components – some more and some less acrimoniously.

In short, the Labor Party called for strengthening social welfare in the USA in the direction of those Western and Northern European countries, where just transition policies were embedded within existing welfare policies. Equally importantly, by placing the environment squarely within this programme, it was one of the early proponents of ecosocial welfare among labour unions.

Domestically the union sought to diffuse just transition within the labour, environmental and environmental justice movements. In late 1996, despite the opposition of the United Mineworkers, the American Federation of Labor and Congress of Industrial Organizations (AFL-CIO) established a working group[8] to bring unions and environmentalists closer together. Negative reactions to the Kyoto Protocol by fossil fuel unions hampered this effort, particularly the formulation of a comprehensive labour-environmentalist agenda that included just transition (for more on the period, see Renner 2000: 59–71; Stevis 2021c; interviews).

The OCAW also played a critical role in the creation of the Just Transition Alliance (JTA) in 1997, evidence of the influence of the emergent environmental justice movement (Dreiling 1998; Gottlieb 2005 Harvey 2018; interviews). The JTA brought together environmental and social justice organizations that represented the most vulnerable and marginalized populations in the USA. In addition to co-developing innovative training initiatives, the JTA and the OCAW collaborated on a number of local campaigns that sought to bring together workers and frontline communities to promote unionization along with environmental justice (Public Health and Labor Institutes 2000; interviews). The collaborations were not always successful but they were programmatic. The JTA still exists and played a key role in the formation of the Climate Justice Alliance in 2013, thus providing a direct link to the origins of the just transition strategy.

In addition to its domestic efforts, the OCAW also emphasized international politics. In particular it collaborated and had a direct influence on the Canadian Communications, Energy and Paperworkers Union (CEP) (part of which used to be the Canadian arm of OCAW and for which Brian Kohler worked). The CEP adopted a just transition resolution in 1996 with the OCAW following suit in 1997. In 1999, the Canadian Labour Congress (CLC) adopted a just transition resolution followed by a fairly detailed programme of action in an ultimately unsuccessful effort to push Canada towards an ambitious climate policy (CLC, 2000; Bennett, 2007; interviews). The OCAW also developed connections with elements in the British labour movement working on occupational safety and health (see *Hazards* magazine; correspondence with participants) and was in

---

[8] First called the Climate Change Group and, after 1999, the BlueGreen Working Group.

contact with the Spanish Comisiones Obreras (CCOO), which were developing an ambitious labour-environmentalist agenda and who played a major role during the subsequent period.

The statement of the International Confederation of Free Trade Unions (ICFTU) at COP3 in Kyoto (1997) argued that 'workers will demand an equitable distribution of costs through "just transition" policies that include measures for equitable recovery of the economic and social costs of climate change programmes' (ICFTU, 1997: 1). In November 1999, the International Federation of Chemical, Energy, Mine and General Workers' Unions (ICEM), where the OCAW was active, adopted a just transition resolution at its second world meeting. A report by Winston Gereluk and Lucien Royer (2001), who coordinated labour's environmental affairs at the global level, particularly at the UN Commission for Sustainable Development (UNCSD), clearly considered just transition as part of labour's agenda.

During this first period, there was very limited academic research (Cohen-Rosenthal 1997; Cohen-Rosenthal, Fabens and McGalliard 1998; Bennett 1999) or applied research (Powers and Markusen 1999; Barrett 2001; Barrett et al. 2002) on just transitions (but there was growing research on labour environmentalism), and the two were tightly coupled in the sense that the authors were both researchers and practitioners. A forum where questions of just transition were more likely to appear was the journal *New Solutions*, which Mazzocchi had helped set up as a research arm of the OCAW's efforts.

The Decline of Just Transition in the USA

Existing divisions among unions and between some unions and some environmentalists became deeper as climate policy rose in significance, bringing an end to the effort of the AFL-CIO's working group to fuse 'jobs and environment with just transition'. The OCAW could not do much to stem this tide because, in early 1999, it merged with an anti-environmentalist union that was not supportive of its priorities and ultimately ceased to exist autonomously (interviews).

While labour-environmentalist collaboration continued and grew, the strategy of just transition was not part of it. In the views of some unionists active during that time, manufacturing unions avoided the term because they saw it as too defensive and preferred a 'jobs and environment' narrative. Others point out that unions in the energy sector were opposed to the very idea of a transition. And still others point to the opposition by the generally conservative US unions to the democratic socialist vision within which the OCAW sought to embed just transition. In any event, the term practically disappeared from US union politics and remains a controversial term to this date.

The 'jobs and environment without just transition' approach, currently dominant in the USA and a number of other countries, was exemplified by the United Steelworkers, one of the largest manufacturing unions, which as early as 1990 recognized that climate change was real and existential and that unions ought to address it as a challenge and an opportunity (USW Environmental Task Force 1992 [1990]; Stevis 2021c; interviews). In addition to climate change, the union was also alarmed over the impacts of automation and offshoring on manufacturing and unionization, manifested in socially unregulated trade agreements. In this they were joined by other unions as well as environmentalists who argued for the inclusion of labour and environmental clauses in trade agreements. During this period, the USW developed relations with environmentalists and after the collapse of the AFL-CIO working group, they proceeded to create the BGA (2006), which continues to be very active. While it does address equity in transitions, it has not made just transition a central component of its strategy because it alienates many unions, including some of the BGA's members.[9] During the early years of the millennium, this approach was also supported by the Energy Task Force of the AFL-CIO, which proposed an 'all of the above' energy approach to temper opposition to climate policy and just transition within the organization. Through their efforts they were able to persuade the AFL-CIO to stop blocking the efforts of the International Trade Union Confederation (ITUC) to adopt a climate programme, as I will discuss in the next section (interviews).

Closing Comments on the Emergence of Explicit Just Transition

This brief historical account suggests a number of lessons. First, the focus on the USA is due to the fact that the explicit *term* 'just transition' was first used here. As I have sought to highlight, the USA is neither the origin of labour environmentalism nor the origin of implicit or embedded just transitions. Second, labour environmentalism and just transition were affected by the dynamics of the overall political economy, which gives capital much more power than it gives unions, environmentalists or communities. Third, while positionality in the political economy does inform the responses of unions, these responses are influenced by strategic choices, ideology and the strategies of business and states. Some of the major supporters of labour environmentalism and just transition have been unions that were in the extractive

---

[9] There was some evidence during late 2022 that this is changing, perhaps motivated by the massive climate policy of the Biden administration, which reflects BGA priorities and also includes significant environmental justice and 'just transition' funding (without using the term; Stevis 2022).

and manufacturing sectors. Fourth, the general parameters and divisions within labour environmentalism are already evident, but the differences between the 'jobs versus environment' and 'jobs and environment' framing do require a more nuanced clarification. The OCAW was in favour of a green industrial policy within a broader democratic socialist welfare platform. On the other hand, the BGA's strategy has and continues to centre on green industrial and infrastructure policy that is indirectly embedded in a social welfare vision. This tension – between a just transition as a major social welfare reform and just transition as a collateral result of green growth – remains to this day around the world. In my view, this is as important a debate as the 'jobs versus environment' or 'jobs and environment' debate. During the next period, from 2001 to the present, we see an effort by global unions to fuse the jobs and environment strategy with explicit just transition in the face of a neoliberal crisis and social democracy's increasing inability or unwillingness to respond to it (Przeworski 2021).

3 The Globalization of Just Transition: 2001–Present

On 11 September 2001, there was a planned meeting, at AFL-CIO headquarters, between US unions and environmentalists participating in the working group discussed in the previous section. The goal was to bridge the deep divisions that had already stalled this effort to bring labour and environmentalists together around an ecosocial agenda that included just transition. The terrorist attacks kept the meeting from happening and the group disbanded. Yet, by 2015 just transition had, symbolically, reached the heights of world politics. The period from 2001 to the present can be divided into three sub-periods. From 2001 to the end of 2007, just transition would be referenced in various labour-environmentalist initiatives, both national and global, but not as the main narrative. Beginning in 2008, it became the major labour-environmentalist narrative at the global level through the fora of climate negotiations. And since 2015, it has spread well beyond labour.

The Globalization of Labour Environmentalism: 2001–2007

During the first decade of this millennium, there was a significant move towards globalizing labour environmentalism. Critical players in this effort were the ICFTU and the Trade Union Advisory Committee of the OECD and a growing global network of labour environmentalists (Rosemberg 2010, 2013, 2020; interviews). Central to this network were the Spanish Comisiones Obreras but, also, the Global Labour Institute at Cornell as well as labour environmentalists from UK, Canada and Continental Europe (interviews).

The environmental turn of the CCOOs is one worth highlighting (CCOO 2006; Gill 2013; Martin Murillo 2013; discussions with principal leader). Starting during the late 1980s, the union internalized environmental priorities and attended climate and other negotiations. Among its major accomplishments were the election of environmental stewards in the workplace, the inclusion of environmental provisions in collective agreements and the establishment of a major research institute. With respect to global labour environmentalism, the formation of Sustainlabour, a labour-environmentalist NGO, in 2004 can be considered a turning point. Sustainlabour focused on a broad range of environmental issues, in addition to climate change. Most importantly, and in increasing collaboration with global union organizations and IGOs, it set out to promote labour environmentalism around the world with particular attention on the Global South (Sustainlabour and UNEP 2008). This resulted in the 2006 Trade Union Assembly in Nairobi (UNEP 2007) with a second one in 2012 in Buenos Aires. The 2006 Assembly is considered to be a turning point in terms of participation by unionists from around the world, in terms of its broad labour-environmentalist visions and in terms of deepening labour–IGO collaboration, particularly with UNEP and the ILO. Yet, while the concept of just transition was employed in the work of Sustainlabour, as well as during the 2006 conference, it did not have the centrality that it subsequently took (for an overview, see Rosemberg 2020).

Global union organizations are weak confederal entities which must work within the parameters of their stronger affiliates (Stevis and Boswell 2008; Stevis 2020). However, there is variability among them and it is often the case that global policy entrepreneurs, in collaboration with like-minded national unions, can influence the narrative and, sometimes, the practice of national unions. In addition, global union organizations have formal access to some IGOs, particularly the ILO and the OECD, and have managed to situate themselves as labour's voice in additional IGOs, such as UNEP or the UN Commission on Sustainable Development, as well as global negotiations, such as those about the climate or the Sustainable Development Goals.

Up to 2006, the US AFL-CIO had been able to prevent global union organizations from adopting a climate agenda, not to mention one that included just transition. Around that time, some US labour unionists associated with the organization's Energy Task Force were able to include elements of just transition within its agenda, in exchange for a broad approach to the energy transition to include 'all of the above' forms of energy (Rosemberg 2020; Stevis 2021c). These policy entrepreneurs brought the US labour movement back into climate negotiations and tempered its opposition to the strategy of just transition – at least at the global level. This allowed the newly formed ITUC – the 2006 result of the unification of the social democratic/social liberal ICFTU, the Christian World

Confederation of Labour and a number of national communist unions – to also engage just transition (on global union politics, see Stevis 2020). A turning point was the 2007 Bali conference when the US unions threw their weight behind climate policy and just transition, leading global unions to make the inclusion of just transition into the negotiated text a strategic goal. In 2008 the ITUC and other participating unions were recognized as a separate non-governmental category for the first time and after significant effort. During that same year, the ITUC and national unions set up a Task Force on Energy that provided the forum for intra-union negotiations on the issue (see Rosemberg 2020; Thomas 2021; interviews).

Another important development during these years, and one that crossed over to the subsequent period, was the emergence of climate justice and efforts to connect it to just transition (Evans 2007; Long, Roberts and Dehm 2010; Guerrero 2011; Tokar 2018). Australian environmental/climate justice activists noticed that Australian unions started using the concept, and out of it came the first systematic study that paid close attention to the social and environmental dimensions of just transition (Evans 2007, 2009, 2010). This project is indicative of the increased attention by environmental justice/climate justice advocates to the concept of just transition outside the USA and the Just Transition Alliance. These efforts accelerated during the latter parts of this decade. By 2015 climate justice as well as just sustainability scholars and activists (e.g., Swilling and Annecke 2012) had engaged just transition and, in the case of the USA, this led to the formation of the Climate Justice Alliance in 2013.

Long March through the Institutions: 2008–2015.

Over the next eight years – from the Bali COP of 2007 to the Paris COP of 2015 – labour unions, coordinated by the ITUC, were able to place just transition on the global climate agenda, if not make it part of climate policy (ITUC 2009a, 2009b). During this period, climate and sustainability justice activists joined labour environmentalists in promoting the concept. The adoption of the ILO's Guidelines for a Just Transition (ILO 2015) and its symbolic inclusion in the Paris Agreement opened the gateways to its proliferation – a question addressed in the next historical section.

Just before the Great Recession, and following the success of the 2006 Trade Union Assembly in Nairobi, the ITUC along with UNEP and the ILO launched a collaborative project and commissioned a report on green jobs, drawing upon the work of the Worldwatch Institute (Renner, Sweeney and Kubit 2008),[10]

---

[10] Michael Renner had long advocated the green jobs. An early critical approach, still a standard in my view, is the work by Kate Crowley (1999), which also reflects Australian union interest in the subject.

which came out as the Recession was unfolding and addressed just transition extensively, as distinguished from a proliferation of Green New Deal proposals that, unlike today, did not prioritize just transition nor work and workers (see Tienhaara 2014; Stevis, Morena and Krause 2020: 17–18).

Trade unions that were engaged in the climate process pushed for the inclusion of just transition in United Nations Framework Convention on Climate Change (UNFCCC) decisions and proposals to highlight the benefits of decisive climate action for workers and their communities.[11] As a result, just transition was increasingly framed and recognized as the trade union movement's contribution to the international climate debate. In a flyer produced in the lead-up to the 2009 Copenhagen climate conference, the ITUC presented just transition as 'a tool the trade union movement shares with the international community, aimed at smoothing the shift towards a more sustainable society and providing hope for the capacity of a "green economy" to sustain decent jobs and livelihoods for all' (ITUC 2009b: 1). For the ITUC, the aim of just transition was to 'strengthen the idea that environmental and social policies are not contradictory but, on the contrary, can reinforce each other' (Rosemberg 2013:19). Just transition also represented a way of mainstreaming environmental issues within the union movement and building bridges with other – especially environmentalist – actors engaged in the international climate debate (Hampton 2015; Morena 2018; Rosemberg 2020).

By shedding light on the social implications of climate change, just transition filled an important gap in the international climate debate. The priority for many climate justice activists involved in and around the UNFCCC had been to get industrial countries to recognize their historical responsibilities for climate change and to act upon them – both through more ambitious national mitigation efforts and through higher levels of financial and technological assistance to less industrial countries. When climate justice groups referred to the uneven social impacts of climate change, they tended to focus on geographical differences. Limited attention was paid to the differentiated social implications of both climate change and climate policies on the world of work in both the Global North and South (JTRC 2018).

Despite differences among global unions, as well as opposition, labour environmentalists sought to integrate some kind of just transition within global climate politics (Räthzel and Uzzell 2010; Felli 2014; Stevis and Felli 2015; Thomas 2021). These efforts started delivering results with the 2013 adoption of just transition by the ILO to be followed by its 2015 guidelines. Another was the willingness of some environmental and climate action organizations to engage

---

[11] This and the next paragraph draw from Stevis, Morena and Krause (2020).

labour and the strategy of just transition before 2015 and the Paris Agreement. The inclusion of just transition in the preamble of the agreement, symbolic as it remains, and its encouragement that just transition proposals be included in Nationally Determined Contributions (Glynn et al. 2020) can be considered the result of global labour environmentalism, a factor often misunderstood by analyses that place the origins of just transition in 2015. Moreover, the synthesis that this network proposed is closer to that of 'jobs and environment with just transition', albeit one influenced by the liberalization of environmental politics over the last several decades.

The efforts of global unions, led by the ITUC, were possible and impactful because particular national unions were increasingly connecting environmental policies with just or social transition, albeit in different ways. The European Trade Union Confederation (ETUC 2007), the Australian Metal Workers Union (2008) and the Trades Union Congress (TUC 2008) were early movers. Some progressive South African unions debated the concept and developed training for their members during the early years of 2010s advancing an ecosocialist approach (communications with participants; Cock 2011). It is worth noting that labour environmentalists from liberal capitalist countries – such as Canada, the USA, the UK and Australia – paid particular attention to the strategy during those early years perhaps because, like the OCAW, they saw it as a strategy to defend and deepen the limited social welfare policies in their countries (interviews and communications). By 2015, just transition had become part of the agenda for a significant number of labour environmentalists, some climate and environmental justice activists, and the ILO. If there were other entities that had adopted explicit just transition I have not been able to find them. After 2015, the use of, and research on, explicit just transition has exploded.

Diffusion of Just Transition: 2015 to the Present

In this last section, I will briefly map the proliferation of explicit just transition across social forces, including, now, explicit just transition policies (Felli 2014; Caldecott, Sartor and Spencer 2017; Just Transition Centre 2017; JTRC 2018; Stone and Cameron 2018; Morena, Krause and Stevis 2020; Pai, Harrison and Zerriffi 2020; Pinker 2020; Atteridge and Strambo 2021; Clarke and Sahin-Dikmen 2021; Heffron 2022; WRI 2022).

At the level of global unions, the ITUC (e.g., 2017, 2021), the International Transport Workers' Federation (ITF 2022) and Public Services International are the most supportive. IndustriALL (2019, 2021) has also adopted the strategy and has expanded its sectoral scope. Regionally the ETUC has long supported just transition with its research arm – the European Trade Union Institute

(ETUI) – going further in its focus on ecosocial politics (e.g., 2021, 2022). The Just Transition Fund (European Commission 2022) has placed the strategy on the agenda of unions in every EU county, in some cases positively and in some cases negatively. Unions throughout the rest of the Global North are engaging the concept, if not without tensions. In the USA, most unions are opposed or sceptical, but some changes are on the horizon.

The strategy is also increasingly reaching unions in the Global South. As noted, some South African unions were among the earliest, as were some Argentinian Unions. The Trade Union Confederation of the Americas, the American arm of the ITUC, has done so more explicitly through the Development Platform of the Americas mentioned earlier (Anigstein and Wyczykier 2019; TUCA 2020; Nunez 2021). Through the work of ITUC and TUCA, additional Latin American national unions have adopted educational and capacity-building initiatives, such as the Brazilian Central Única dos Trabalhadores (CUT 2021). Just transition remains a profound issue of debate among unions and beyond in South Africa (Satgar 2018a,b; Winkler 2020; Hochstetler 2021; Sikwebou and Aroun 2021). The ITF, in particular, has carried on education and capacity-building initiatives around the Global South (2022). The Global Labour University, an educational collaboration of unions and their allies, is paying strong attention to just transition, particularly its 'Just and Green: Labour's Ecological Question' massive open online course that is attended by unions and unionists from around the world. The Trade Union Network for Energy Democracy (TUED) brings together unions from around the world that support public energy policies and just transition (Sweeney and Treat 2018), and has recently launched a Global South TUED to promote a 'public pathway' approach to just energy transition. It is fair to say, therefore, that just transition is increasingly finding its ways into the agendas of unions in the Global South.

The 2016 launch of the Just Transition Centre (JTC) signalled the beginning of a new phase in the ITUC's just transition efforts – one that reflects a renewed commitment to collaborative industrial relations and social dialogue. The centre's originality lies in its close collaboration with two global green business groups – The B Team and We Mean Business – that are actively involved in the international climate arena (JTC and The B Team 2018). It is worth mentioning that the launch of the JTC coincided with the closure of Sustainlabour, which, as we have seen, was a primary driver of labour environmentalism and just transition at the international level, and, moreover, one with a more ecosocial and Southern focus. The Centre, as well as the ITUC, continue in their efforts to globalize just transition (Márquez, Gil and Maeztu 2019; ITUC 2018; Union to Union 2020; Stevis 2021a; correspondence with union officials).

In addition to the ILO and the UNFCC (2015), other intergovernmental bodies are also taking an interest in the topic, but not always with a focus on workers and frontline communities, and are likely to use 'inclusive' rather than 'just' transition. In 2017, for instance, the OECD commissioned a report on just transition from the newly created Just Transition Centre (2017), while the World Bank started a just transition from coal programme in 2018 (World Bank 2018) and is supporting the Just Rural Transition initiative. The Climate Investment Funds, a multilateral funding mechanism for the Global South, has launched the Just Transition Initiative (2022), which prioritizes South Africa and India and is based on the analytical scheme developed by the JTRC.

The global diffusion of just transition, particularly in the context of the international climate negotiations, has led to the adoption of just transition language by a number of prominent environmental NGOs and networks. Many are now referring to just transition in their campaigns and publications (IISD 2018; The Lofoten Declaration 2017). These include the Sierra Club in the USA, as well as Greenpeace and Friends of the Earth and others, both internationally and nationally. The largest global network of NGOs working on climate change, Climate Action Network International, has also taken an interest in the concept and developed advocacy positions on the topic (CAN 2018). In India, iForest has initiated a just transition research and advocacy project, as well as the India Just Transition Centre (e.g., Banerjee 2021). While Indian advocates are relative newcomers, South African civil society, as well as unions and the government, have been debating just transition as far back as 2010.

In parallel, just transition has also made a noteworthy comeback in the USA, if cautiously among unions (Labor Network for Sustainability 2016; JTLP 2021). At the grass-roots level, community-based labour and environmental justice organizations and networks are actively campaigning for a just transition that is not restricted to labour issues or dirty energy, but also focuses on cultural, gender and racial injustices, and is connected to a general critique of extractive capitalism (Climate Justice Alliance 2017a,b; JTLP 2021).

Other initiatives come from the corporate sector.[12] The reference to just transition in the preamble of the Paris Agreement further legitimized the concept and encouraged a wider range of stakeholders to use it. This was complemented by the concept's compatibility with the agreement's voluntary and bottom-up theory of change and the wider narrative on the combined economic, social and environmental benefits of climate action, especially in the energy field. These include initiatives directly undertaken by companies and

---

[12] This and the next paragraph draw from Stevis, Morena and Krause's (2020).

business advocacy organizations and philanthropies. The relations between the finance sector and just transition have received significant attention (Robbins et al. 2018). The World Benchmarking Alliance is systematically tracking about 450 companies with respect to their social and environmental practices in the transition to a low-carbon economy.

Philanthropic initiatives include the Just Transition Fund in the USA, launched in April 2015 with support from the Rockefeller Family Fund and Chorus Foundation, whose mission is to support Appalachian coal-dependent communities to transition to a strong, resilient and diversified economy (see Morena 2016 and 2022). German political foundations have also been active in the international just transition space. More mainstream climate funders, such as Bloomberg Philanthropies and the European Climate Foundation have also incorporated just transition wording into their work – for example, the Beyond Coal campaigns in the USA and Europe – as have foundations involved in the recently established F20 Platform.

From Advocacy to Policy

Most of the above initiatives, with the exception of some of the work by IGOs, global negotiations and, possibly, some corporations, fall in the realm of advocacy and research. In recent years, however, a number of countries and subnational units have also adopted just transition policies or are engaging in policy formulation, allowing us to move the analysis beyond proposals and into practice. In what follows, I differentiate between adopted policies and policy formulation processes, such as task forces and other administrative initiatives, and limit myself to explicit just transition policies (for more information, see JTRC 2018; Pinker 2020; Heffron 2022; WRI 2022; for the USA, see JTLP 2021). More comprehensive research should definitely include policies that do not use the term but are, for all purposes, aiming at just transition. A detailed examination of whether just transition proposals included in Nationally Determined Contributions have entered the policy stream is also necessary (Glynn et al. 2020).

There are not that many explicit just transition policies, yet. These include the European Union Just Transition Fund and the related policy edifice, the Coal Plan in Spain, the Ruhr transition policies, transitions in the Latrobe Valley in Australia, the just transition from coal in Colorado, the energy transition in Illinois, the closing of the Diablo Canyon Nuclear Plant in California and the Huntley Coal plant in New York State, and a few others (see Just Transition Centre 2017 and WRI 2022, which, however, use elastic criteria).

Policy formulation policies are also important in the sense that some governments have decided to set in motion a task force or other process to develop just transition proposals that may be adopted after further negotiations. Here we can include the formation of the Territorial Just Transition Plans in the EU and task forces, or related, in Canada, Ireland, New Zealand, Australia, South Africa and various states in the USA, such as New York State, California and Los Angeles County. Most of these efforts aim at transition out of coal but Scotland's is focusing on oil. I expect the number of policy proposals that employ the term to increase in the near future.

Research Catches Up and Moves Ahead

As just transition has risen in prominence so has applied and later academic literature with clearly different patterns for each sub-period. During the first period there was growing applied research that started appearing towards and immediately after 2007 (e.g., UNEP 2007; Renner, Sweeney and Kubit 2008; TUC 2008) and some academic research (Gould, Lewis and Roberts 2004; Evans 2007).

A research project by Evans bridges the two sub-periods and is the first systematic project to explore just transition and this from an environmental justice angle (Evans 2009, 2010; Evans and Phelan 2016). Another line of emergent research was largely labour-centred (e.g., Rosemberg 2010, 2013; Cock 2011; Räthzel and Uzzell 2010, 2012, 2013; Snell and Fairbrother 2011, 2013; Goods 2013; Hampton 2015). This labour-centred approach has expanded since to accommodate both research on labour unions and just transitions and a broader approach from the angle of environmental labour studies and political economy (Morena, Krause and Stevis 2020; Räthzel, Stevis and Uzzell 2018 and 2021). A third line of work, headlined by Swilling and Annecke (2012), has its own parallel origins in just sustainability and points towards a synthesis of just transformations and sustainability (e.g., Temper et al. 2018; Bennett et al. 2019; Kohler et al. 2019; Newell 2019).

Since 2015, academic and applied research in just transitions has flourished (for systematic reviews, see Wang and Lo 2021; Abram et al. 2022; Wilgosh, Sorman and Barcena 2022; on energy, see Pai et al. 2020). A central thread has sought to connect just transitions and energy transitions, with variable attention to work and workers and the breadth of the just transition strategy (e.g., Newell and Mulvaney 2013; Jenkins et al. 2016, 2018; Healy and Barry 2017; Snell 2018; McCauley and Heffron 2018; Clarke and Lipsig-Mummé 2020; Hochstetler 2021; Newell 2021; Flanagan and Goods 2022). Increasingly, in fact, research on just transitions has focused on different issues areas such as cities (Hughes and Hoffman 2020) design (White 2020), healthcare (Stevis, Morena and Krause 2021), transportation (Schwane 2021; Galgóczi 2019), agriculture (Bastos Lima 2022; Tschersich and Kok 2022), the politics of just transitions (Ciplet and Harrison 2019; Ciplet 2022), law (Doorey 2017; Chacartegui 2022) and just transition in relation to various aspects of and approaches to political economy (e.g., Routledge, Cumbers and Derickson 2018; Cock 2018; Satgar 2018 a and b; Stevis and Felli 2020; Winkler 2020; Galgóczi and Pochet 2022). Again, some of these literatures vary in terms of their focus and interpretation of just transitions. The adoption of policies has also motivated more empirical research around the world (in addition to some of the sources just mentioned, see Goddard and Farelly 2018; Reitzenstein, Schulz and Heilmann 2020; Gutler, Low Beer and Herberg 2021). Some of that growing research will be situated in the sections that follow.

Closing Comments on the Globalization of Just Transition

This section highlighted the role of national and global labour environmental-ists in placing just transition on the global climate agenda and, thus, the reason why most analysts connect it to climate and energy. Second, we are currently witnessing the increasing diffusion of just transition across social forces and organizations. This calls for a systematic analysis of how just transition is used by various social actors. One way is to identify and cluster the many defin-itions and operationalizations of just transition without noting the political differences among them. Another is to recognize that just transition is a contested concept because people and organizations invest it with their own political preferences. The analytical scheme employed in the rest of the Element leans in the second direction and provides criteria that allow us to differentiate just transitions in terms of the social and ecological worldviews embedded in them.

4 The Breadth of Just Transitions

The National Labour Relations Act of 1935 gave workers across the USA the right to unionize. By any measure it expanded political, social and economic rights for millions of unskilled workers in the manufacturing sector and is responsible for the economic growth of the USA during the post–Second World War era. However, it did not and does not cover, among others, inde-pendent contractors, farmworkers and domestic workers – the latter two largely women, black people or immigrants (Perrea 2011). Moreover, the Act did not require the racial and gender integration of unions, leaving that for the 1970s and 1980s and beyond. It is otherwise egalitarian policies like this that motivate the way I approach breadth.

In order to map the inclusiveness of a just transition policy, or any other policy, I employ *scale* and *scope* in the spirit used by Chandler (1994). Scale refers to the spatial and temporal reach of a particular transition or just transition initiative.[13] Scope complements scale by forcing us to interrogate the social and ecological content of scale. In the first part of this section I will elaborate on scale and scope. In the second and longer part I will combine the two and explore the implications by drawing on just transition cases.

The Scales of Transitions and Just Transitions

Spatial Scales

What are the spatial scales in play? First, there is the geographic space of a transition, whether due to decarbonization, artificial intelligence or economic agreements. Research on global divisions of labour, production networks and chains, lifecycles, circularity or telecoupling allow us to identify the spatial scale of a practice with greater specificity, in the process making clear that space is shaped and reshaped by historical human practices (e.g., Bair 2009; Dicken 2015; Boillat et al. 2020). Almost every place on the globe has been affected, socially and ecologically, by global and translocal processes over the last 500 years, and practically every place is currently affected by such processes (Grove 1994; Mann 2011; Marks 2019). For the crafting of effective and just transition policies we need granular information on the social and natural geography of transitions. The geography of the coal production network, for instance, is different from that of natural gas, both in terms of the places and the people affected at particular points in time.

The second spatial scale is the jurisdictional reach of the just transition policy, which, ideally, must mirror the geography of the transition itself. However, as with most policies, just transition policies are limited to particular jurisdictions. At the global level this is consistent with the limited and uneven governance framework that bends in the direction of policies that enable rather than socially regulate capitalism, increasingly so since the 1970s (for historical background, see Murphy 1994; Mazower 2013). For example, the social regulation of global economic agreements through social and environmental clauses has been effectively resisted by corporations and governments, resulting in a patchwork of policies. Nor do we have social regulatory policies accompanying global environmental policies, whether biodiversity, wastes, the climate or even the ozone. The social regulatory governance that we have is limited to often controversial

---

[13] One could use scale and scope to also map a transition in progress against the transition necessary to deal with a problem. Scope does address this to some degree. In any event, this is a key question prior to exploring ongoing transitions.

extraterritorial policies, the work of weaker intergovernmental organizations – such as the ILO, the UN or the World Health Organization – and private societal regulatory schemes (to be differentiated from corporate social responsibility) such as Fair Trade, the Forest Stewardship Council or Global Framework Agreements (Stevis 2010a; Raynolds and Bennett 2015; Auld, Renckens and Cashore 2015; Hadwiger 2018).

The weakness of transnational ecosocial regulatory governance should not be read as the absence of transnational governance, both public and private (Shamir 2011; Phillips 2017; Mayer and Phillips 2017). Domestic policies routinely play a transnational governance role, whether they deal with accounting rules or the use of technology that is considered of national security interest. Economic and military agreements, generally bilateral or minilateral, provide governance on economic and military affairs. Analysts of value chains have long identified the governance role of particular companies. Hybrid organizations, such as the ISO, play a significant role while economic IGOs have entrenched the Global North's dominance in the world political economy. The point is that the effective transnational governance that we have, fragmented and incomplete as it may be, leans in the direction of managing and enabling capitalism and geopolitics rather than social and ecological regulation.

These jurisdictional tensions are not limited to the global level but are also evident at the sub-national level, especially in federal countries. In the USA, they play out in a variety of ways, including climate policy (e.g., Karapin 2016). Research has highlighted both the upward harmonization impacts of superior state policies ('the California effect') and the downward harmonization impacts of inferior policies ('the Delaware effect'; Vogel 1995). On the positive side, California's recent decision to ban the sale of new internal combustion vehicles after 2035 will accelerate the manufacturing of electric vehicles. On the negative side, the policy does not provide a just transition for workers and communities that will be affected. Moreover, it does not prevent a state like Texas from allowing the sale of internal combustion vehicles or encouraging the production of energy for electric vehicles from fossil fuels. While the conflicts within federal systems are the product of domestic politics, the competition between California and Texas does not stop at the borders of the USA but affects the location of international investment. Similar dynamics are evident in other federal countries such as Canada, Australia or India.

Temporal Scales

The temporal scale of a transition reaches into the past and into the future (Adam 1998; Nixon 2011; Davies 2019). Time, along with space, is (re)shaped by historical dynamics, while the temporality of our practices and policies is shaped by how our choices have shaped space. A look at the infrastructures that connect us and divide us leaves little doubt about the spatiotemporal nature of our world (Mann 2011; Bridge et al. 2013; Marks 2019).

Any human activity has a history that is reflected in the ways in which it has organized nature as well as people. Which legacies of the past should be remediated by a just transition policy and on the basis of what criteria? Similarly, work in environmentally dangerous industries is manifested by a long trail of people whose working capability has been interrupted, not to mention the vast numbers of retirees with health problems (Winnant 2021).

In addition to identifying how far into the past a current transition reaches we must also ask how far into the future. Like other industrial and infrastructural activities renewable energy will leave its own ecological and social footprints. What kinds of arrangements do we need to adopt so that turbines and panels do not become the coal mines and oil wells of the future? In short, just transition strategies must also be evaluated in terms of their congruence with the temporal scales of a transition. Most just transition policies have long time frames in terms of their implementation but even these do not align with the historical time frames of the transitions they are responding to. In fact, their time frames are often compromises that delay decarbonization.

A comprehensive transitional policy must combine short and long-term provisions (Cha at al. 2019). Committing vast resources to transitions from fossil fuels to renewable energy, or remediating the legacies of the past without addressing the immediate needs of those affected in the short term, is not a comprehensive just transition. Nor is the temporary expenditure of huge amounts of money to temper pain and suffering, as is the case during various crises. Just transitions require short and long-term resources and these resources have to align with the scales of the transition.

Another important temporal question is whether the just transition policy takes place protectively or proactively (Vachon 2021). A protective policy commences after the transition has unfolded; a proactive is in anticipation of the transition. Proactive policies are preferable, but they are not necessarily transformative. For instance, a proactive policy may focus on green industrial policy or diversification, both desirable, but may not aim at a more egalitarian and ecological political economy (Vachon 2021:119; also Vachon 2023). While it is desirable for transformative policies to be proactive it is also possible to envision more and less ambitious protective policies.

The pace of the transition is also important (Delina and Sovacool 2018; Bond 2019; Newell 2021; Newell and Simms 2021). Many analysts have highlighted the urgency of a rapid energy transition. An urgent transition is desirable but so is a just transition that is commensurate with it (Stevis and Felli 2020). If the urgency of a transition is used to delegitimate questions of power and justice we are entering problematic and empirically weak terrain. There is no compelling evidence that the energy transition has been slow due to demands for justice. The calls for common but differentiated responsibility, desirable as the principle is, have been less about justice and more about geopolitics. A forward-looking global climate policy would need to transfer significantly more resources than those mentioned at COP27 (2022) – in terms of training, technology, finance and more – and over longer periods of time. It would also have to address the rules that cause the inequalities underlying these needs. These inequalities, in turn, cannot be understood solely across countries since the evidence suggests that the emissions inequalities within countries are often as serious as those across countries (Kenner 2019; Oxfam 2020; Chancel 2021).

The Scopes of Transitions and Just Transitions

A few years ago, a popular Greek-Albanian artist complained publicly that his mother's pension was lower than that of Greeks with the same years of service. The public reaction was one of indignation on the grounds that Greece had an obligation to treat Greeks of the diaspora as well as mainland Greeks. That obligation, however, did not include the hundreds of thousands of Albanian immigrants in Greece who do not receive the same benefits for the same work. This story is at the heart of the distinction that much of liberal, statist and communitarian international relations theories employ between insiders and outsiders, and highlights the need to pay close attention to scope as well as scale. Moreover, as with scale, we need to pay close attention to the alignment of the scope of the transition and the just transition policy, including in terms of adequate and appropriate resources.

As noted in the historical sections, explicit just transition policies were not originally associated with climate politics but, rather, with logging and toxins, although Mazzocchi was aware of the significance of climate change early on. The association with climate is the result of its rising significance, as well as a strategic choice by unions. Increasingly, labour environmentalists and others argue that just transitions are needed for any transitions whether food, health, biodiversity, manufacturing, cities, transportation and other (e.g., IndustriALL 2021; Anderson 2021a,b). In a recent project, we heard of the need to address all unjust transitions, including those due to liberalized trade as well as the changing nature of the workforce (JTLP 2021).

This brings me to the next layer of scope. Just transitions must cover all affected, including across value chains and production networks (Young 2000,

2006; Reitzenstein et al. 2018). Difficult as this seems we already have a great deal of research, if not enough results, on upgrading labour and environmental rights across jurisdictions (e.g., Barrientos, Gereffi and Rossi 2014; Dicken 2015; Boillat et al., 2020). Just transitions limited to some of those affected will result in negative externalizations and force those left out to seek their own solutions. However, this is only one way in which affected parties can be left out. Sectors and occupations are historically associated with categories of people (Burke and Stephens 2018). Most energy workers are males and, in the USA, white males. Most nurses are women while most physicians in certain specialties are men. In short, focusing on particular industries means focusing on particular categories of workers. While we can argue that a just energy transition is central to climate policy, it is difficult to use that as an argument against addressing other transitions without reproducing existing gender, racial or other inequalities. However, even within the energy sector there are profound divisions of labour with men doing certain jobs – for example, running nuclear plants – while women and immigrants do the service work associated with these plants.

But a socially comprehensive policy may leave nature out or include it selectively. For example, the closing of a coal plant may not remediate either the plant or the coal mines involved (e.g., Wang et al. 2022). When dealing with just environmental transitions, this gap is apparent but it becomes increasingly less so as we move towards transitions not conventionally considered as environmental. In my view, all social policies are also environmental as all environmental policies are also social. Healthcare, for instance, accounts for about 10 per cent of emissions globally. Changes in the provision of health care will certainly affect them, not to mention the use and disposal of single-use medical supplies (Stevis, Krause and Morena 2021).

Expanding the Scope of Just Transitions

Just Transitions for All Transitions?

A recent project in which I participated made the need for just transitions across all transitions abundantly clear and highlighted that allowing unjust transitions to unfold with respect to automation, economic liberalization or any other transitions breeds a politics of insecurity and resentment, including against environmental transitions (JTLP 2021). In fact, there is nothing that intrinsically limits just transitions to environmental transitions as there is nothing that limits ecosocial welfare to some aspects of the ecosocial. Clearly a comprehensive just transition policy will meet with significant opposition, in the same way that comprehensive health and education policies have. However, although that does happen unfortunately, we do not prioritize some diseases or some students in pursuing socialized education or health care. To paraphrase Herman Daly (Marchese 2022), the move from ad hoc views of just transition (or healthcare or education) requires changes in the fundamental design of our political economy.

Arguably all social welfare policies can be thought off as just transition policies. One of the major demands of the socialist and labour movements of the nineteenth century, for instance, was that of a 'just transition' from working age into old age. Another was a 'just transition' from the ability to work to inability to do so due to injury. In these, and other cases, workers, soldiers, widows and their allies (Skocpol 1995) argued that society owed them rights and protections because of their contributions over their working years – something similar to the argument made by coal workers today. Yet, even though implicit or embedded just transition policies are common in social welfare countries, it is important to note that adding ecosocial welfare policies is not automatic, as France's further move to nuclear power and Norway's fitful transition from fossil fuels demonstrate (Houeland and Jordus-Lier 2022).

Just Transitions from, Just Transitions to, Just Transitions in

All transitions from something are also transitions to something. This is particularly evident with the transition from fossil fuels to renewable energy. Advocates of 'jobs and environment' have extolled the multitude of green jobs that can absorb many more workers and heal communities (Daneker and Grossman 1979; Pollin 2018; IRENA 2021). However, transitions *from* are not necessarily transitions *to*. Many of the workers that are transitioning from the past are too old, or do not have the appropriate skills, or do not have the means to move. Many of the thriving resorts in Colorado used to be mining towns but miners and their families were forced out by the absence of work and high property taxes. Moreover, much of the new labour force cannot afford to live in the towns in which they work while nature has been repurposed to fit new economic activities rather than restored (Park and Pellow 2011). A transition that does not help the specific workers, communities and places affected is an economic development or diversification policy but not a just transition policy.

The need to pay close attention to the coupling of just transitions from the past and into the future is evident by the serious problems associated with renewable energy (Mulvaney 2013, 2014; Zabin et al. 2016). Renewable energy's ecosocial practices are not particularly exemplary, whether that is workers' rights, the mining of minerals, production or siting (Davidson, 2023).

But just transitions are not only necessary for transitions from the past and into the future. They are also appropriate for industries that are neither new nor declining yet are going through transitions (Anderson 2021a,b). One of the most pressing issues in the USA, for example, is that of elder care (Winnant 2021). The growing number of older people requires ever more care workers, mostly African American and immigrant women who are not well paid nor enjoy workplace protections and rights. It is telling that one of Joe Biden's social infrastructure proposals, now failed, was to invest $400 billion over eight years to enhance the wages and rights of elder care workers and the quality-of-life of their patients (Stevis 2021b; Bigger et al. 2022). A just transition, in fact, is also necessary in the case of the social welfare economies that are proud of their health systems. Most of them depend, to a significant degree, on immigrants from the Global South – ranging from custodial staff to nurses and physicians (see Bludau 2021; Stevis, Krause and Morena 2021). A strong argument can be made that the Global North owes reparations to the Global South and that the global health system requires a massive just transition policy.

Questioning the 'Private'

Historically, the fact that the environmental transition has been driven by public policies raises an important conundrum. Do public policies provide a moral ground and an opportunity to associate transitions with the power and legitimacy of the state and the public good? What about transitions due to corporate decisions? Shifts in employment and investment irrevocably affect the broader public, leading the state to provide a safety net and/or contain discontent. However, a 'private' transition is not public only because of its social impacts and costs. Behind all private economic activities lie significant public expenditures, including research and education, training, procurement and all kinds of other incentives and disincentives (Bairoch 1993; Block and Keller 2011; Mazzucato 2015; Mayer and Phillips 2017). The current competition by eponymous US billionaires over who will build spacecrafts for NASA is an example. Not only are these crafts built on technology produced by public means but, also, the funding for building and deploying them is public. Because 'private' choices have public origins and impacts, their naturalization strengthens the private domain and weakens the public sphere.

From Heteronomous to Autonomous Just Transitions

The previous discussion expanded the universe of just transitions. Can we go any further? Must just transitions be triggered only when a transition – however we delineate it – commences? Does such an approach render just transitions heteronomous by leaving out transitions from capitalism, colonialism, racism, patriarchy, nativism, extractivism, anthropocentrism and all social and eco-logical inequalities? Can we envision just transitions as an autonomous and generative policy that initiates the transition itself? In Section 6 I suggest that the more ambitious a just transition is the more it is part of more egalitarian and ecological political economy that addresses both transitional challenges and deep-seated inequalities. Throughout history, in fact, egalitarian transitions are driven by a desire to both eliminate inegalitarian practices and move towards egalitarian ones.

While justice is integral to just transition (see next section) the empirical interface between (environmental) justice and just transitions will vary depend-ing on whether we adopt a more heteronomous or autonomous approach to just transitions. If we assume that just transitions are in response to ongoing transi-tions, then just transitions are a segment of justice. On the other hand, if we adopt an autonomous approach whereby just transition policies are necessary to move us from unjust arrangements, then the overlap of justice and just transi-tions increases significantly.

Fusing Scale and Scope

The focus on both scale and scope helps render visible all those affected, whether included or excluded by a just transition policy. Why is it local, national or global? Why does it deal with legacies of the past but not future risks? Why does it cover frontline workers but not service workers in the same plant or industry? Why does it include or exclude corporations in the allocation of burdens? Here I would like to suggest some configurations of scale and scope and illustrate them with just transition examples (see Figure 2)

A well-known just transition policy involves the closing of the Diablo Canyon Nuclear Plant in California (JTLP 2021; interviews). The original plan was to decommission the plant by 2020 but that was delayed to 2025 as part of a compromise that would help workers transition to retirement or other employment.[14] After pressures the original plan was modified to include more support for non-frontline workers as well as the community that would lose the tax income from the plant. The closing of the plant is not related to a broader strategy of abandoning nuclear energy in California or the USA. In fact, the main union in the plant is a strong supporter of nuclear energy and the union and the company agreed to not fight the decommissioning any further because the plant had become too large for the company's needs – because of the increasing use of renewables. As a result it is not a model that can be used in other nuclear plant

---

[14] It is now moved to the 2030s, because renewable energy has not grown as rapidly as expected.

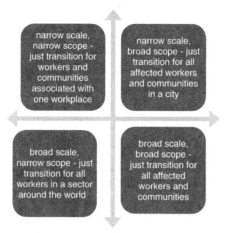

Figure 2 Fusing Scale and Scope

closures. This does not mean that the just transition agreement was not necessary, humane and useful. Rather, its scale and scope were limited as a result of political exigencies. Even so, it is evident that the policy could have been broader or narrower in scope. A very narrow option would have only included the operators who were members of the main union, while a much broader option would have included all workers as well as the local community and the many consumers of the energy produced by the plant (the direction in which the transition moved).

The State of Colorado has adopted the first sub-federal just transition from coal energy in the USA and the world (unless we consider the Ruhr case to be sub-federal) (Colorado 2022; BlueGreen Alliance 2021; interviews).[15] A motivating factor was the adoption of a decarbonization policy by the state. Yet, there is no reason why a just transition strategy would have been the answer. In fact, when the state raised its Renewable Energy Standard in 2010, some of the participants involved in shaping the just transition policy were opposed to it (Betsill and Stevis 2016). This time around, an alliance between environmentalists, environmental justice communities and labour environmentalists persuaded hitherto hesitant unions to join. Yet, this alliance was not strong enough to also call for a just transition in natural gas and oil, both much more important than coal in Colorado, nor prohibit the mining and export of coal. The end result is a detailed just transition plan that focuses on coal miners, coal plant workers and railroad workers. It does not include service and other workers, nor does it provide for the disproportionally affected communities subject to persistent environmental and social injustice. It does envision

---

[15] For a comparison of the two, see www.pocacito.org/beyond-fossil-fuels/beyond-fossil-fuels-just-transition-in-colorado-and-germany/.

significant attention to coal communities affected by the closing of plants and mines. Its approach, in fact, is fairly broad in that it treats them as places that should be desirable for people to stay or move to. Yet, so far, the policy does not prevent communities with more human resources to apply for and get most of the funding, funding that should go first to the most marginalized communities.

The transition from coal in Canada is likely to cover the whole of the country (Mertins-Kirkwood 2021; Brown and Jeyakumar 2022; Canada 2022). In fact, Canada recently banned the exportation of thermal coal (coal for energy production, the largest use of coal). Yet, coal is a very small part of Canada's energy mix, employing very few people, while it is not clear that the transition process has included all affected, particularly women and Indigenous people (Mertins-Kirkwood and Deshpande 2019). So here we have a just transition that is national in scale but limited in sectoral and social scope, and does not provide a blueprint for a comprehensive transition that will include oil from tar sands and nuclear power.

In the case of Spain's Plan de Carbon (Spain 2018), considered as a good example of how workers will be transitioned, the scope is slightly broader than Canada's because coal's share in Spanish energy production is higher – but still quite small compared to other sources. Yet, the plan covers only plants that are declining while exempting those that are doing well. However, it must be noted here that Spanish unions as well as the current social democratic government have larger just transition ambitions. One example of that is the establishment of Institute for the Just Transition within the Ministry of Ecologic Transition and the Demographic Challenge.

The European Union's Just Transition Fund (Sabato and Fronteddu 2020; European Commission 2022) and the edifice within which it is envisioned (European Commission 2019), is an example of a spatially broader policy that remains narrow in scope, as the EU recently designated natural gas and nuclear power as sustainable. Even though there are certain deadlines, the reality is that both sources of energy are likely to become part of a much longer 'transitional' process. A fuller evaluation of the European Just Transition Fund and related policies will have to await the development and implementation of the envisioned Territorial Plans, which may be more or less inclusive albeit unlikely to totally modify the limits of the fund (see Rösch and Epifanio 2022).[16]

The case of South Africa is a good example of the tensions between transitions from coal and transition into renewables (Bond 2019; Sikwebu and Aroun 2021; Hochstetler 2021; South Africa 2022; correspondence). Over the last

---

[16] The Just Transition Info site is useful for tracking these plans, particularly with respect to Eastern Europe – www.just-transition.info/reports/.

decade or so, there has been a major debate over a just transition from coal and the role of the country's main energy provider, Eskom. Metalworkers and others have been engaged in this discussion and have pointed out that Eskom, a public company, is privatizing itself and the country's energy system. This it is doing in various ways including making its energy transmission arm a separate company so as to better facilitate private renewable energy producers. Here, therefore, is a major disagreement between unions and management – with the former supporting a public energy system and one that provides decent and unionized employment. The recent report of the Presidential Commission on Just Transition has met with significant criticism, particularly with respect to its ecosocial provisions (Satgar et al. 2022; South Africa 2022; communication with unionist). Moreover, it is not clear that the Just Energy Transition Partnership, decided at COP26, to finance and spur SA's transition is sufficient and appropriate.

Closing Comments on Breadth

While global climate negotiations target fossil fuels and their uses, the move from coal seems to be the common denominator of most local or national just transition policies with the exception of Scotland and some local initiatives. In a general sense the world is going through an uneven transition from coal, and that is a problem in terms of climate policy. Moreover, in the absence of a global just coal transition policy, uncoordinated and in fact competing local or national just coal transitions may well result in downward rather than upward harmonization. So, we can say that the global and the local or national just transitions from coal are seriously mis-aligned and that is likely to happen with oil and natural gas, if we get to them.

These dynamics are not simply the result of jurisdictional arrangements. Rather, jurisdictional arrangements are employed or challenged by social forces, whether from a position of weakness or power and whether to advance or prevent certain preferences (Sassen 2005; Mezzandra and Neilson 2012). This is important to highlight because these contestations are embedded within power relations that are translocal, even in the case of nativist neoliberalisms of the types emerging in the USA, Brazil, Poland, Russia or India. None of these countries is proposing a break from the world political economy. Rather, their goal is to reposition themselves in it. A global just transition will require national just transition policies that do not export their costs. The rise of nativism adds urgency to this but even promising national proposals, like various Green New Deals, have been properly criticized for not paying serious attention to their global implications (Zografos and Robbins 2020; Kolinjivadi and Kothari 2020a,b; Schumacher 2021).

5 The Depth of Just Transitions

One of the more celebrated ecological transitions of the last two centuries has been the creation of parks and related natural areas (Grove 1994; Macekura 2015; Alexander 2023). Transitions to natural areas can protect ecosystems from large-scale extractive processes such as mining, logging and industrial agriculture but they frequently dispossess the working poor and Indigenous people who depend on access to these areas (e.g., Paddock 2022). Political ecologists are increasingly sensitive to that possibility and have called for just conservation (Vucetich et al. 2018; Wienhues 2018; Pichler at al. 2022). Another celebrated success has been that of occupational health and safety. Workers have long sought safe and health workplace conditions (Slatin 2009; Turk 2018). Some unions and professionals limit their concerns to the work-place while others have sought to place workplace conditions within a broader environmental politics (Bennett 1999, 2007). These two brief examples under-score the challenge of fusing the social and the natural.

From Social and Ecological Inequality to Ecological Justice

Just transition policies may be very broad in scale and scope – yet shallow in terms of their social and ecological goals and the necessary and appropriate resources to carry them out. The discussion that follows centres around social and ecological inequality and thus foregrounds power by some humans over other humans and over nature. On that basis I propose a typology of environmental justice and just transitions that fuses nature and society (Hopwood, Mellon and O'Brien 2005). This diverges from the polyvalent (recognition, participation, distribution, restoration) and sectoral (energy, climate, food, etc.) approaches in that it emphasizes the mutual constitution of these dimensions and sectors within the historical political economy in which they occur. Debates over political, economic, social, cultural and environmental rights were an earlier iteration of the polyvalent approach (Moyn 2019). Liberals, broadly construed, focused on rights as separate domains, as we can do with dimensions of justice. Social democrats, also broadly construed, placed rights within their effort to create a social welfare state while democratic socialists, also broadly construed, placed rights within their effort to create a socialist society (for a useful effort to align dimensions of justice with overall political purpose, see Schwane 2021; for a broader account, see Przeworski 2021).

Gradational versus Relational Approaches to (In)equality

The debates between relational and interactional ontologies have a long history, including in international relations. Only relatively recently, however, have they become the subject of study (Jackson and Nexon 1999; Trownsell et al. 2019).[17] Relational ontologies are central within historical materialist and historical structuralist views (Ollman 1977, 2015; for an application to labour environmentalism, see Jordhus-Lier, Houeland and Ellingva°g 2021). During the early part of the twentieth century, socialists argued that national politics was taking place within a world political economy that countries, in turn, shaped (e.g., Bukharin 1973 [1915]). Beginning in the 1940s, the Global South argued that its subaltern position was not due to traditionalism but, rather, unequal global divisions of labour (Frank 1966; dos Santos 1968). The solution, in turn, was the reform or overthrow of uneven and constitutive North–South relations, as argued by dependency theories. The Global North rejected these demands while by the 1990s the leaders of the Global South had joined global capitalism (Stephen 2014; Nayyar 2016). The Global South had moved from a relational to a gradational or interactional approach to (in)equality in Erik Olin Wright's (2016) language.

Relational ontologies imply that inegalitarianism, whether among humans or between humanity and nature, is the product of relations that constitute the parties to those relations. The parties are not ontologically separate entities whose interactions ultimately determine how harms and benefits are distributed among them, as would be argued by interactional/gradational approaches, including liberal constructivists whose use of relations falls within interactionism. According to the latter, inequality is based on the innate or acquired differences among various entities – humans, social categories or countries and so on. There can be different interpretations of the relational and interactional/gradational approaches but the key difference is central. Undoing relational inequality requires both the redistribution of harms and benefits and the reorganization of the power relations integral to them. On the other hand, gradational/interactional inequality requires measures that enhance the better distribution of opportunities and benefits. In dealing with just transitions the distinction between relational and gradational inequality is useful. From the latter perspective, just transitions would enhance the opportunities and resources of those affected but would not undo the power relations among them. From a relational vantage point, a just transition would be an opportunity for reforming or transforming those power relations. Placing just transition within the quest for an egalitarian ecosocial society reflects a relational approach in the sense that the goal is to transform the rules within which just transitions take place. This is important because the explicit just transition

---

[17] Here we could add organismic (e.g., Gaia) and functionalist (e.g., socio-ecological systems) ontologies, both of which are quite prominent in environmental debates.

proposals from business, IGOs, government and many civil society organizations aim at regulating the interactions between unequals, rather than changing the power relations among them.

Social and Ecological (In)equality

A common means to capture attitudes towards nature is in terms of the anthropocentrism-ecocentrism continuum (Low and Gleeson 1998; Hopwood, Mellor and O'Brien 2005; Schlosberg 2007; Clapp and Dauvergne 2011; Dryzek 2022). At one extreme, we can place approaches that see nature as a resource to be used until its depletion. Further along, conservationists seek to replenish natural resources, whether for hunting or fishing, or other forms of extraction, such as logging. Ecocentric approaches extend intrinsic value to nature although there are differences in how that takes place. Deep ecologists may do so by downgrading the standing of humanity while social ecologists seek a synthesis of society and nature, allowing for an exploration of the interfaces between social and ecological criteria and values.

Yet, it is necessary here to avoid assuming that, somehow, the ways in which we know and value nature are independent of our relational inequalities and differences – whether one comes from an ecocentric (e.g. Celermajer at al. 2021) or an ecosocialist vantage point (e.g., Malm and Warlenius 2019; Moore 2019). In my view, non-human nature cannot, yet, provide us with unmediated information on how this can be done (Stevis 2000). Accordingly, all approaches towards nature involve adjudicating among different human views on the matter. To point out that society and nature are constituted within an internal relationship should not leave the impression that they both have equal agency, anymore than slaves and slaveowners did or workers and capitalists do. This is not to pass judgement on the 'agency' of nature (Colle and Frost 2010; Gamble, Hanan and Nail 2019) but, rather, to foreground, how power relations among humans shape power relations between humanity and nature (on power, see Avelino 2017).

On the basis of this discussion, I propose the following synthesis (see Figure 3). Inegalitarian and anthropocentric views are likely to produce injustice and unjust transitions while egalitarian anthropocentric views are likely to produce environmental justice and just transitions – seen in terms of environmental harms and benefits. Inegalitarian views that privilege nature – whether deep ecology, biocentrism or preservationism – will produce ecological injustice and unjust transitions, as would be the case with the transition to natural parks around the world, while egalitarian and ecocentric views are more likely to produce ecological (or socio-ecological or ecosocial) justice and just transitions. Social equality is a necessary if not sufficient condition for ecological justice or equality, if you

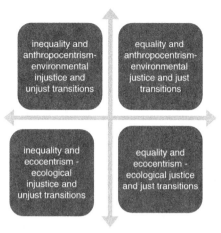

Figure 3 Configurations of social and environmental inequality and justice

wish. On the other hand, social inequality is necessary and sufficient for environmental/ecological injustice or inequality, unless one fully separates the social and the ecological. Varieties of justice and just transitions fall in the two quarters on the right in Figure 3. In the next sub-section, I outline varieties of environmental and ecological justice and just transitions. I would like to reiterate here that while from an interactional ontology, justice could take place by providing more resources to the less powerful, from a relational ontology this could require the simultaneous increase in the power of the weak and decrease in that of the powerful. Such changes would require a recalibration of state–society and society–nature relations.

Varieties of Environmental Justice in Just Transitions

According to Low and Gleeson (1998), environmental justice refers to justice between humans while ecological justice refers to justice between humanity and nature (also Schlosberg 2007; Pellow 2018; for various relevant chapters, see Coolsaet 2020). In what follows I propose a typology that differentiates between weak and strong environmental justice and weak and strong ecological justice (Ehresman and Stevis 2018). This four-way typology suggests that environmental and ecological justice fall along a continuum, rather than in discrete categories, while it allows for the differentiation among just transition policies and proposals in terms of their social and ecological priorities.

Weak environmental justice deals with the unequal distribution of environmental harms and benefits as another aspect of justice among humans and without, necessarily, eradicating the systemic sources of these injustices. In the case of coal, for example, just transition may be paid by exporting coal or other fossil fuels. In the case of pollution it may lead to moving an activity or adopting adaptation measures.

The empirical record suggests that most just transition policies, so far, fall within weak environmental justice and some may not clear that hurdle (Caldecott, Sartor and Spencer 2017; Atteridge and Strambo 2021; WRI 2022). Their social justice goals are limited to addressing the problems of some workers and communities, important and necessary goals, but do not address the organization of the sector or the whole political economy. Their environmental goals are limited to the reduction of emissions by closing a plant or mine without remediation (Wang et al., 2022). The Colorado just transition policy does address some environmental justice issues but, for the most part, these are the subject of a totally different policy. The Diablo Canyon plant decommissioning was motivated by the concerns of environmentalists over the impacts of nuclear power. However, that was not a major concern of the unions or communities involved. Their primary, and valid, concerns were about the interruption in their lives that would emerge from the transition. The European Union Green Deal seems to include both but that is misleading in the sense that the green and just parts do not necessarily affect the same places.

Strong environmental justice also treats injustice as an issue among humans but does aim at the eradication of the causes behind environmental injustice (Shrader-Frechette 2002; Farrell 2012). Strong environmental justice can employ a precautionary approach that protects nature, even if it does not give it explicit standing, while also limiting the discretion of the most powerful. Labour environmentalists, social environmentalists and community activists promoted strong environmental justice during the 1970s (Rector 2014). A number of analysts have argued that weak environmental justice became dominant in the USA during the 1980s and 1990s (Pellow and Brulle 2005; Holifield, Porter and Walker 2009; Harrison 2014; Purdy 2018) leading to calls for a critical environmental justice that takes nature into account (i.e., ecological justice; Low and Gleeson 1998; Pellow 2018).

There are no just transition policies that fall within strong environmental justice. However, there are cases in which strong environmental justice concerns have been raised. In the South African debates, for example, environmentalists and some unions advocated the reorganization of the energy sector in a manner that is socially more egalitarian and diminishes emissions and other environmentally damaging activities (Satgar et al. 2022). The unsuccessful Proposition 1631 in Washington State also advanced a strong environmental justice agenda that included marginalized workers and Indigenous people in its decarbonization vision (JTLP 2021). In fact, one could argue that it included some strong ecological elements.

Ecological justice extends standing to nature, a significant and challenging expansion of justice. Weak ecological justice extends protections to some aspects of nature and some of the people affected, managing coupled socio-ecological systems without addressing ecosocial inequalities. Pricing ecosystem services would fall within this category as would preservation policies that protect some habitats and spaces in exchange for the use of the rest as resources. Strong ecological justice, on the other hand, addresses both the symptoms and the causes of ecosocial inequalities. Significantly, strong ecological justice was first developed during the early 1970s under the term 'eco-justice' (Hessel 2007). Eco-justice proposed a holistic view of humanity and nature as part of the 'creation' while arguing against social inequalities– a demand motivated by the emergence of a naturalist ecocentric approaches that cast justice in terms of an undifferentiated contrast of humanity and nature.

There are not, yet, just transition policies that fall within the weak ecological justice category even though there are many ecological inequalities. However, as debates over (un)just biodiversity and conservation transitions grow, weak ecological just transitions are possible (Agarwal 2001; Paddock 2022; Pichler et al. 2022). Similarly, there are no strong ecological justice just transitions but there are proposals that aim in that direction. The first systematic research project on just transitions that I have found – that dealing with the Hunter Valley in Australia from around 2006 to 2010 – was motivated by a desire to fuse social and ecological justice (Evans 2010). Some social environmentalists, such as Friends of the Earth in the Scottish case, have advanced what could be considered a stronger ecological justice approach in the sense that they pay close attention to workers and communities, as well as the society–nature nexus. The European Trade Union Institute (2021), moving beyond its parent – the European Trade Union Confederation – has linked just transitions with a turn towards an ecosocial political economy, and has engaged the interface between just transitions and degrowth (ETUI 2022). The Trade Union Confederation of the Americas also offers elements of an ecosocial agenda (TUCA 2020). A number of the Green New Deal proposals during the last several years lean in the direction of embedding just transition within an egalitarian ecosocial political economy (Cha et al. 2022; Schumacher 2021). However, the debates over Green New Deals are illustrative of the different approaches to justice and just transitions (e.g., Zografos and Robbins 2020).

Procedure *and* Substance

During the last several decades the polyvalent approach has sought to provide a more diverse set of lenses (recognition, participation, distribution, restoration), reflecting discomfort with the silences of justice research (Schlosberg 2007, 2013; for chapters on these dimensions, see Coolsaet 2020), and has been applied extensively to the analysis of just transitions (Jenkins et al. 2016, 2018; McCauley and Heffron 2018; Pai, Harrison and Zheriffi 2020). However, while the approach enriches our study of environmental justice it risks the reification of the various dimensions into different forms of justice that are the product of their particular characteristics rather than those of the broader political economy (see Fraser 2017). My view is that these dimensions are relationally constituted and can best be understood within the broader political economy, as has been the case historically. For example, industrial relations involves recognition, participation, distribution and restoration (the latter in the case of healthcare, disability and retirement, for example). As already noted, during the late nineteenth and first part of the twentieth century there was another polyvalent approach – separating political, social, economic, cultural and human rights (Moyn 2019) – and parties combined them into distinct political programmes (see also Adereth 2021). This is not to say that the polyvalent and sectoral justice approaches are not analytically and substantively useful, as has been the case with regime analysis in international relations, but they do demand that analysts decide on whether each dimension and sector is ontologically distinct or whether they intersect within common historical relations of power and inequality (i.e., whether they lean towards a relational or interactionist ontology).

Inclusion as an Incomplete Measure of Egalitarianism

In the previous section, I explored who is covered by just transition policies as a first approximation for inclusion (Stevis and Felli 2020). Even so, inclusion is not always an indicator of empowerment. As Agarwal (2001) and others have suggested, inclusion may well lead to participatory exclusion (i.e., to being included as a means of containment rather than empowerment (Gaventa 1980; Cox 1981). Some collective agreements between unions and businesses have included just transition provisions, but these cover unionized workers only while they are employed. A similar situation can occur when we treat categories of people as homogeneous. It is not uncommon, for instance, to place labour unions within the left even though labour unions range significantly in terms of ideology. The Polish union Solidarity, for instance, is quite conservative and is collaborating with the US right-wing think tank Heartland. Market-leaning environmentalists, such as the Environmental Defence Fund, have close relations with business. Finally, a particular category of people may be empowered in ways that do not challenge systemic inequality. Liberal feminism or liberal antiracism can well lead to the emancipation of women or other categories within the parameters of capitalism (Fraser 2017).

Distribution as an Incomplete Measure of Equality

During the second part of the nineteenth century, von Bismarck pushed through pensions for workers, against the resistance of capital and aristocracy in order to stem the rise of socialism (see Boissoneault 2017; Sacks 2019). After the US Civil War the victorious Republicans transferred enormous amounts to veterans and their widows but refused to make that a permanent part of the US social safety net (Skocpol 1995). Modern corporate social responsibility has also shifted significant resources towards society and, in some cases, select categories of workers (Kauffman 2004).

In recent years the world has expended enormous resources on the Great Recession and the pandemic. The 2022 energy crisis, induced by Russia's invasion of Ukraine, led Germany to nationalize a key energy company and the EU to tax the excessive profits of fossil fuel companies. However, none of these policies reflect a permanent shift towards egalitarianism. By comparison, the expenditures envisioned by the various just transition policies and proposals are modest, largely because most transitions are limited to coal and, even then, not in major coal-producing or consuming countries.

Voice and *Choice*

In order to address the possibility of participatory exclusion I approach participation in terms of both voice – the right to engage in deliberations or negotiations – and choice – the kinds of options that can be deliberated or negotiated (Stevis 2002; Tapia, Ibsen and Kochan 2015; Bayles, Bogg and Novitz 2018; Pulignano and Waddington 2019). My argument is that by examining voice and choice as part of procedure I can highlight that procedure and substance are mutually constituted. The first question about voice is whether the just transition policy includes all those affected (i.e., whether the scope of voice is commensurate with the scope of the transition; but see Ciplet and Harrison 2019). This is particularly relevant for informal, contract or unwaged workers as well as workers and communities up and down the value chain. Broad voice does not guarantee a strong choice. Narrow voice ensures that some will be left out.

The second question is the strength of the voice that the various participants have. This is an important empirical question because there are forms of voice, such as robust industrial relations and social dialogue, that enable significant participation by select groups of workers, albeit within definite parameters of choice. As noted, the 1950 collective agreement between the United Autoworkers and GM (Treaty of Detroit) legitimated the right of unions to negotiate wages, healthcare and pensions that were attached to employment in a specific corporation while leaving out hiring, location, production and automation decisions. This division of power has proven detrimental to workers and unions since the 1970s. Currently, global union organizations and unions in coordinated capitalism promote the value of strong social dialogue in shaping all policies, including just transitions (Just Transition Centre 2017; Ferrer Márquez et al. 2019). However, a closer look at industrial relations at the level of the European Union, where social dialogue is important, reveals that it ranges from the most common symbolic information sharing to the much less common joint agreements that bind corporations at the EU level (Pulignano and Waddington 2019). The inclusion of some unions, and thus some workers, in the deliberation and implementation of just transition policies in Colorado, Canada, EU, Illinois, South Africa or Spain is positive but, also, incompletely inclusive if it does not increase the voice and choice of workers and diminish the voice and choice of capital.

Consistent with this, voice and choice are performative if those that are relationally or gradationally privileged can abstain, with their abstention insulating them from social regulation (on limits to wealth, see Robeyns 2019; on climate inequality, see Kenner 2019; Oxfam 2020; Chancel 2021). The impact of the subaltern is stronger if those in power have to participate in a policy process that can well result in choices that diminish their power. Increasingly, finance has been very concerned about climate risks and, more recently, just transitions (Robbins et al. 2018; London School of Economics 2022). To the degree that representatives of unions and environmentalists (even liberal ones) participate in such deliberations, they do so as observers rather than decision makers. In my view, then, stronger choice and voice for the subaltern requires the weakening of the voice and choice of the powerful (i.e., a reorganization of power relations).

In my empirical research on just transitions I have come across evidence of the uneven and selective extension of voice and choice during the crafting of policies. In one case, for instance, the voice of workers did not include coal miners. This was due to the lack of organization on their part but, also, to the fact that coal can continue being exported. The disproportionally affected communities did participate but did not have much voice or choice in the process. A key reason for that was the understanding that the policy would target workers in coal plants and coal transportation as well as coal communities. Those workers had significant voice but within the parameters of mandated decarbonization and with the understanding that the envisioned resources were not guaranteed because the jurisdiction at hand could not raise its taxes. The point is not to criticize those involved, but to state that their voice had to be exercised within limited choice.

Closing Comments on Depth

My goal in this section has been to place varieties of just transitions within social and ecological (in)quality and power. On that basis, I proposed a continuum from weak environmental justice to strong ecological justice rather than categories based on the polyvalent or sectoral approaches whose analytical potential I fully appreciate. The analytical scheme employed here allows me to associate particular types of environmental or ecological justice with particular types of ecosocial politics. The just transition policies and policy proposals around the world are both a small portion of transition proposals and fall largely within weak environmental justice, reflecting the hegemony of neoliberalism and associated crisis management. However, there are also proposals from social environmentalists, including labour environmentalists, that point in the direction of strong environmental justice and even strong ecological justice. At this moment, it is not clear to me that any government, corporation, intergovernmental organization or negotiating fora are open to proposals for strong environmental or ecological justice.

6 The Ambition of Just Transitions: A Double Take

One of the crown jewels of the European welfare state is healthcare and a substantial number of the workers in the sector are skilled and unskilled workers from Eastern Europe and the Global South (Bludau 2021). The depth of the social welfare provided depends on a breadth that extends well beyond European countries – with no obligation towards the countries of the immigrant labour force. From a different point of view, nativist parties sincerely (or not) pay tribute to the social welfare state by associating it with the nation, which they feel is besieged by immigrants of certain kinds.

I distinctly recall a US steelworker, whose company was shutting down, recounting his visit to Brazil when its unions and companies were becoming major players in the steel sector. While discussing union solidarity, he was surprised when a Brazilian union member told him 'now you are in our place'. He realized then how narrow the strategy of US unions had been when most of steel production was in the USA. To this day, steel and auto manufacturing unions in the USA, Germany, Brazil and other industrial countries are trying to find common ground against both company policies and their own nationalist policies. More recently, the Biden administration's green industrial policies, welcome by a number of unions and environmentalists, are reproducing these geopolitical tensions (Stevis 2021b; Bigger et al. 2022).

Both examples demand that we examine breadth and depth before deciding on the ambition of a strategy or a policy. In the first sub-section of this section, I discuss why it is necessary to examine the articulations of breadth and depth in a world political economy that is organized around divisions of labour that constitute and situate actors and where dominant worldviews and institutional arrangements routinely differentiate between insiders and outsiders (O'Neil 2000; Kukathas 2006; Young 2006; Schaeffer 2012).

Breadth *and* Depth: The First Take

Figure 4 identifies a range of configurations of breadth and depth. At one extreme, we can very well have a local just transition or other ecosocial welfare policy that is comprehensive and even inclusive of all local stakeholders but thatexternalizes harm by exporting emissions while importing the minerals required for renewable energy, generally extracted under socially and ecologic- ally harmful conditions (Davidson 2023). These negative externalities are likely to lead to downward harmonization (or race to the bottom) as each locality is striving for advantage.

Alternatively, a local just transition that absorbs the costs of the transition (e.g., leaves coal in the ground and assists both the coal producers on which it has

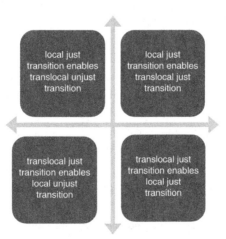

Figure 4 Breadth and depth: the geography of (un)just transitions

depended as well as the producers of the minerals needed for renewable energy) can lead to collaboration and higher translocal standards. This is clearly a high bar, particularly when the just transition policy is at the level of a plant or a sub-federal unit, especially in a poorer country. Yet, the fact that cities and other local entities adopt aggressive green strategies to attract certain kinds of investments indicates that translocal policies are the result of political contestations rather than a 'natural' outcome (author's personal observation from serving on a city climate advisory committee). Local just transition politics, like all other kinds of ecosocial welfare policies in liberal political economies are challenging but, also, possible (for urban just transitions and justice, see Hughes and Hoffman 2020; Janos and McKendry 2021; C40 2022). Adopting just transition policies at the level of a major country, of course, will have profound implications around the world, provided that it is not a cover for geopolitical goals such as the climate tariffs that the USA and the European Union want to impose on imports and which point to China (Stevis 2021b).

The third category involves intersections of breadth and depth that use whole countries or undifferentiated categories of people as the unit of analysis. There is good evidence that industrial countries have produced more environmental damage than less industrial countries, and the rise on the agenda of reparatory obligations at COP27 was long overdue. There is also good evidence that a great deal of the emissions in the Global South must be credited to the Global North because they are the result of Northern investment (Kenner 2019; Oxfam 2020; Chancel 2021). These are definitely elements that must be taken into consideration. However, we must also consider two additional elements. First, there is significant emission inequality within countries of the Global North and the Global South and, second, these inequalities are sometimes higher than North–South inequalities. Accordingly, just transition policies that are organized around countries or categories of people as the unit of analysis obscure and reinforce internal inequalities.

Aligning translocal and global ecosocial policies with national policies is a major challenge that requires the close study of existing experiences. The debate over the Common Heritage of Mankind during the Law of the Sea negotiations in the 1970s is a useful case on the problems of aligning global and national justice (Shackelford 2009; Michelson 2019). The politics of the inclusion of labour and environmental standards in economic agreements can provide us with important lessons about the alignment and misalignment of multilateral and national policies (Lechner 2016; Smith et al. 2020). Climate and biodiversity negotiations have been rich sources of information from the very beginning. The Fossil Fuel Non-Proliferation Treaty proposal can also serve as a testing ground for aligning global and national just transitions (The Fossil Fuel Non-Proliferation Treaty 2022).

The goal of this part has been to highlight the need to place the depth of any policy within the world political economy. It is not my view that all local policies – whether just transition or not – have the same translocal reach and impacts. I consider that to be an empirical question. It is also not my view that all local or national policies are shaped solely by formal position in the world political economy. It would be difficult to equate discriminatory nativist, national socialist or fascist welfare policies with the more inclusive social liberal, social democratic or socialist welfare policies. My goal here has been to reflect on who and what is included and excluded, empowered and weakened, even by seemingly admirable mobilizations and policies so as to guard against militant particularism (Williams 1989; Harvey 1995; Gough 2010).

From Opportunities to Rights: The Second Take

Transitions and Transformations

Transformations can move us in any one of many directions, depending on preferences and political power. The world could well move towards nativism or eco-authoritarianism – both transformative changes. Or it could move towards complete decarbonization through nuclear power and geoengineering. Here, and in most discussions the measures of just transitions and transformations are social and ecological egalitarianism, if in varying ways and degrees (e.g., Bennett et al. 2019; Temper et al. 2018; Kohler et al. 2019; Scoones, Stirling et al. 2020; Abram et al. 2022).

With that in mind, the contrast between transitions and transformations seems motivated by the relatively apolitical literature on socio-technical systems transitions (SST). There is nothing that says that just transition could not be connected to the SST approach, deepening the latter's focus on politics and justice (Smith et al. 2005; Meadowcroft 2011; Geels 2014; Newell 2019). However, just transition in substance and language emerged before SSTs, and not as a response to it or influenced by it. One of the few early analysts of labour environmentalism and just transition did try to combine it with socio-technical systems analysis (Cohen-Rosenthal 1997), an approach that was used after the Second World War in a project on work process and work relations in UK coal mines (Trist and Murray 1993), but not with socio-technical transitions that were emerging in the 1990s (Kemp 1994), and were even more technocratic.[18]

---

[18] Here it is worth noting that another debate on transitions, much more attuned to socioecological dynamics, also started during the 1990s. The Great Transition Debate was initiated by the Stockholm Environmental Institute and the Tellus Institute and continues to our day (Raskin et al. 2002).

The prominence of the SST approach may explain why a number of authors differentiate between transitions and transformations. Accordingly, transitions are considered as marginal changes to be contrasted to more profound transformations (e.g., Eckersley 2021). As noted in Section 2 the original just transition proposal was embedded within a rather transformative democratic socialist programme whose goals were broader and deeper than most current Green [New] Deals (Labor Party 1996).

In my view we do need to differentiate among just transition policies and proposals to ascertain which ones are intended to reproduce inequalities or manage crises and which ones aim towards a more egalitarian the political economy/ecology. However, I prefer to use the term 'transformative' in an adjectival fashion for three reasons. First, because some just transition proposals, including the original one, can be transformative; second, because differentiating between more and less transformative transitions is easier than differentiating between more and less transformative transformations; and, third, because I believe it is theoretically and practically important to investigate the staying power and impacts of less than transformative policies. This is all the more necessary since explicit or implicit just transitions, as argued throughout, have emerged within the long-standing conflicts between authoritarian, liberal and socialist politics that have characterized national and world politics since the early nineteenth century. In that sense, transitions or transformations must also be placed within this historical context rather than examined as movements from one ahistorical equilibrium to another.

Hopwood, Mellor and O'Brien (2005) consider policies and views that combine social egalitarianism and strong ecocentrism as transformative. Reformist policies fall lower along both axes and, finally, status quo politics fall very low in both axes. The Just Transition Research Collaborative (2018) modified this approach with particular attention to inclusion, as discussed in the first part of this section (also Krause et al. 2022). In what follows I modify the JTRC scheme by placing the ambition of just transitions within the ambition of the broader political economy that they advance. My goal here is to highlight the fact that ecosocial syntheses vary, particularly since the ecosocial language has attracted some attention recently by both academics and practitioners (e.g., Raskin et al. 2002; Koch and Fritz 2014; Duit, Feindt and Meadowcroft 2016; ETUI and ETUC 2021; Galgóczi and Pochet 2022).

Neoliberal Just Transitions

Liberal environmentalism is present across all walks of life – among unions, environmentalists, parties, states and of course corporations. The common denominator of neoliberal policies is that of opportunities and commodification (for a comprehensive account, see Barbier 2022). Within these parameters there are some important observations worth making.[19]

Neoliberal policies can be as coercive as would be any other type of policy. And they do involve the state – whether enabling or managerial (Bairoch 1993; Block and Keller 2011; Mazzucato 2015). This is important to keep in mind because evocations of innovation and the market tend to naturalize neoliberalism and place it outside politics. Cap and trade, for example, is such an example in the sense that, once adopted, it becomes binding like any other policy. Similarly, Biden's August 2022 climate policies combine neoliberal priorities with an enhanced role of the state in what I call problem management policies (Bigger et al. 2022).

As noted, the finance sector has shown interest in just transitions (Robbins et al. 2018). Finance is especially concerned about risk but some financial actors may also act out of a deeper commitment to corporate social responsibility (JTC and The B Team 2018). However, there is also the potential for gain. An example of a neoliberal financial strategy is that of the securitization of 'stranded' fossil fuel assets as a way of paying for a just transition, as has been the case in Colorado. This policy may well solve the absence of adequate public funds, because of a revenue constraining policy, by commodifying just transition.

Neoliberal policies would be similar whether they are in the USA or Sweden but their implications would be different (Krause et al. 2022). In the USA they would affirm a more humane liberal capitalism if informed by corporate social responsibility. In Sweden, on the other hand, they would undermine the social welfare state to the degree that they shift policy making to the private sphere. To capture this difference I feel that it is better to call them neoliberal rather than status quo or business as usual, a term I have also used.

Just Transitions as Problem Management

This category denotes policies whose goal is to suspend or manage (limit or modify) the expected operation of the dominant political economy to deal with a major tension or crisis.[20] Accordingly, such policies would also look different in a liberal capitalist compared to a coordinated capitalist country. An example

---

[19] I do not discuss philanthropy here but consider it to be a neoliberal strategy (on climate philanthropy, see Morena 2022).

[20] Problem management policies are also used by social welfare or authoritarian regimes to stabilize their operations. I am replacing here the earlier term 'managerial' used by the JTRC to prevent confusion with uses that focus on the role of managers (see Eagleton-Pierce and Knafo 2020).

of suspension would be the US GI Bill for (mostly white) veterans that was adopted immediately after the Second World War. A few years later, when support for the New Deal had declined, it would have been impossible.

Problem management transitional policies with some equity provisions are often adopted during a major crisis, whether the Great Recession, the pandemic or the war in Ukraine. Significant resources are spent to keep the economy going and, often collaterally, contain suffering and unrest. Generally, the protections are episodic, needs-based and inadequate. The defeat of President Biden's social infrastructure proposals in the USA demonstrates, that while large, the responses to the pandemic remain temporary and that the order of things has not changed significantly (Stevis 2021b; Bigger et al. 2022; Cha et al. 2022; Stevis 2022). The EU Just Transition Mechanism may be placed here to the degree that its goal is EU-level cohesion and the containment of resurgent nativism in Eastern Europe, where coal plays a major role.

A more systemic type of such a policy is what has been called green Keynesianism (e.g., Blackwater 2012; Tienhaara 2018). While the state plays an important role, the goal is to stimulate the economy and provide leadership to capital during a major crisis– whether the Great Depression or post–Second World War reconstruction. Green Keynesianism – usually at the national level and thus properly associated with green industrial policy – is prominent in various parts of the world. In the USA, it has been promoted by those unions and environmentalists associated with the BGA and the 'jobs and environment without just transition' approach. At present, many labour environmentalists in manufacturing and other strategic industries around the world are motivated by a green industrial policy approach with significant protectionist elements in it.

Reformist Just Transitions

An important question is whether social liberalism and green Keynesianism with social priorities fall within problem management or reformist social democratic welfare politics. Public education has been a major priority for social liberals, whether to ensure skilled workers or more participation and legitimacy. Protections for widows or retired people as well as basic health care would also fall in this category. In current decades it is represented in Amartya Sen's capabilities approach and a number of related elaborations (for and overview, see Robeyns and Byskov 2020; also Biermann and Kalfagianni 2020 for general context). The basic argument here is that reformist just transition policies require substantial resources that will provide those affected with the capabilities to be agents in the transition that affects them. In my view, to the degree that such policies involve entitlements (the term originally used by Sen) and rights, they move us in the direction of structural reforms by challenging capital's autonomy. When capability policies are not relational (i.e., they do not expand the public sphere and limit the power of capital), they remain within social liberal and social democratic reforms. To the degree that they refer to opportunities and selective protections, they fall within neoliberal and problem management policies. The just transition in the Ruhr, for instance, can be considered as a reformist just transition because it expands, however unevenly, Germany's social contract rather than advancing structural reform. But quite possibly, one could consider it as a problem-solving transition since Germany seems to have made natural gas a main source of energy while it has not been able to temper the energy demands of its car industry.

Structural Just Transitions

Structural just transitions refer to the significant, if not total reorganization of the political economy, to the degree that they expand the public sphere and decommodification in a systematic and substantial manner. In that spirit, a comprehensive just transition fund for all – like healthcare for all – could conceivably qualify. It is perhaps ironic that I am using the term here in the same way that global economic organizations employed 'structural adjustment' to defeat national development and welfare policies while nurturing neoliberalism from the 1980s onwards (Babb 2005). The social welfare state is a major achievement of the social democratic and social Christian movements of the last two centuries. While the boundaries between some social democratic and social liberal reforms are often murky, one cannot dismiss the achievements of strong social welfare states, particularly if one has been exposed to their absence. Yet, it would be risky to assume that social welfare states are automatically steps to stronger ecosocial states – rather than historical formations with their own goals and against a stronger egalitarian and ecological political economy. The history of the bitter debates between social democrats and socialists is well known, while many of the more recent innovations adopted by social democratic states, such as Denmark's flexicurity, intend to advance rather than diminish capitalism.

This brings me to an important question among current advocates of transformative transitions, a question whose history goes back to the late nineteenth century. During the late nineteenth and early twentieth century, the socialist movement was torn apart by disagreements over reform and revolution, an issue that re-emerged during the 1960s in terms of reformist versus 'non-reformist' reforms (see Gorz 1968 [1967]; Bond 2008). These debates recognized that social welfare policies are not simply steps towards a more transformative political economy but can be ends in themselves, as is widely recognized by analysts of varieties of capitalism and social welfare states, among others (see Esping-Andersen 1990; Hall and Sockice 2001; Esping-Andersen and Myles 2014; Frieden 2020; Adereth 2021).

Transformative Just Transitions

Transformative just transitions move us in the direction of a comprehensive egalitarian public sphere in which much of social exchange is decommodified and based on rights and entitlements, and embeds humanity within nature. In terms of justice they move us beyond strong environmental justice between humans to strong ecological justice between humans and between humanity and nature. Arguably, one can differentiate between more and less transformative policies, provided that they reflect a shift in the fundamental design of the political economy, in Daly's words.

Anticipated by the reformist policies in social democratic societies, it is reasonable to argue that such a shift would eliminate stand-alone just transition policies because they will become part of the social welfare state. This does not mean that there will not be serious disagreements over the proper ways to proceed; for example, Green New Deal or Degrowth (Pollin 2018; Hickel and Kallis 2019), Universal Basic Services or Income (e.g., Gough 2019), global divisions of labour (Kolinjivadi and Kothari 2020a,b; Zografos and Robbins 2020) and others. However, these disagreements will be within a different political economy (Wright 2013).

Are there examples of just transition proposals or mobilizations that point in a transformative direction, or at least towards structural reforms. There are several organizations that advance such a worldview including unions, such as the International Transport Workers' Federation (Anderson 2021a,b). The platform of the Trade Union Confederation of the Americas (2020) also includes significant elements, as do the CCOO (2020), while the ETUI (2021) has been exploring the elements of an ecosocial society based on rights. Various social environmentalist organizations are also leaning in that direction (e.g., Greenpeace International and Friends of the Earth, International as well as local chapters, such as FOE Scotland), as do some climate justice organizations, such as the Climate Justice Alliance (2017a,b). What we lack, in my view, are strong political parties, in addition to strategic or tactical coalitions, that challenge the state–society relations at the heart of the political economy. This requires that we do not consider states and societies as ontologically distinct – with the former inherently undemocratic and the latter inherently democratic.

7 Conclusions

Agency and Ambition

The ambition of a just transition, or any other policy, is based on the organizational and political resources of its advocates and opponents. These resources, in turn, are both instrumental and structural. No matter how well organized a union is in the USA, the result will be within the parameters of liberal capitalism, unless liberal capitalism itself is regulated or constrained. This is not only because the USA is a liberal capitalist country, but also because a liberal capitalist country is based on the creation of liberal unions and environmentalists. Some of these unions were made liberal – as was the case with US manufacturing unions after the Second World War, when the left was purged by law. Others were liberal from their very inception, aiming to get their 'fair' share out of capital (on US industrial relations, see Hogler 2004; more broadly, see Kaufman 2004).

Why would a union, community or environmental organization accept a neoliberal or problem management just transition policy? One answer is that it is the best they could get. Multinational corporations may offer just transition as part of their corporate social responsibility agenda to engage their workers. Or a community can deny an offer, leaving them with nothing, or can accept it, thus further legitimating corporate hegemony. Moreover, unions, environmentalists and communities may, in fact, advocate for neoliberal or problem management just transitions because they very much believe in them or find them strategically preferable. The union behind the Diablo Canyon Nuclear Plant, for example, agreed to its closure, but also supports nuclear power around the country. Closing the plant was not a threat to its broader priorities. Similarly, some environmentalists support natural gas – if methane emissions are minimized – so supporting decarbonization from coal, but not from gas, is consistent with their views.

The literature on sustainability transitions properly focuses on the struggles between incumbent and insurgent coalitions (Hess 2014, 2019; Geels 2014; Jenkins et al. 2018). The focus on coalitions, as differentiated from actors, recognizes that power is distributed across social actors. Fossil fuel capital, related state elements, workers and communities benefitting, and so on form powerful and diverse coalitions against change (Betsill and Stevis 2016; Ougaard 2016; Turnheim and Sovacool 2020). Similarly, renewable energy companies, state agencies, their workers and their communities also form countervailing coalitions.

Yet, incumbent and insurgent coalitions are never those of equals, particularly if they are hegemonic. As discussed in Section 2, explicit just transition emerged as a result of 'job blackmail' that disciplined workers, communities and states. The most recent flourishing of corporate social responsibility and social dialogue/multistakeholderism should not hide the fact that they legitimate the authority of capital. Coalitions, in short, involve a range of participants but arrange those participants asymmetrically, with some being more central than others (Stevis and Assetto 2001; Newell 2019; Hess et al. 2021). Considering these arrangements is necessary for systematic empirical analysis.

The second question is whether we can derive the social purpose of a coalition by simply identifying the general categories of participants (e.g., business, environmentalists, unions, communities, states and so on), and the general direction of their efforts (e.g., green economy or just transition). I believe that such an approach can provide some answers but at a precarious level of generality. In the case of Colorado, for instance, the coalition behind the 2010 Renewable Energy Standard was successful by avoiding a climate policy and leaving out natural gas (Betsill and Stevis 2016). This allowed anti-climate constituencies to join the coalition because of the profits to larger farmers from the siting of wind farms, while neutralizing the opposition of natural gas. The state adopted a decarbonization goal ten years later and only after the political balance had changed. Still, natural gas is not part of its just transition policy, postponing that conflict.

This leads me to argue that in examining just transitions, or any other policy, we need to pay attention to the social purpose of competing coalitions (Hultgren and Stevis 2020; Newell 2019). Even during crises, a fuller and more accurate understanding of the politics of green transitions must attend to the composition and internal power dynamics of competing coalitions and, thus, the social purpose that they have negotiated among themselves. Explanations that do not pay attention to the power relations at play and the social purpose of these coalitions are likely to equate neoliberal transitions with egalitarian ones, a great disservice to both research and practice.

Reflections

The goal of this Element has not been to provide a comprehensive discussion of all aspects of just transitions. The politics of policy and the adequacy of policy resources are, in my view, central issues, but I have limited the discussion to the interpretation and comparison of just transitions in terms of their eco social purpose, as this comes out of breadth, depth and ambition. This is not only a 'normative' choice – although it is that as well. It is also a practical choice in the belief that we need analyses that identify the purpose of policies – who they empower and who they weaken and how – in order to better understand their implementation and impacts as well as the political dynamics that produced them (e.g., Ciplet 2022). This allows us to do history backwards, as Bertell Ollman (2003) has suggested, in order to understand the dynamics that connect present and past.[21]

With respect to breadth, I have sought to highlight how the politics of spatial and temporal scale can fruitfully complicate[22] our study of transitions – and any other policies. I have also sought to broaden the scope of just transitions. The approach adopted here is one that considers not only what we conventionally consider transitions, often technological. It also calls for more attention to transition due to policies such as economic agreements or automation, and demographic shifts due to gender and racial emancipation. It goes beyond just transitions as responses to ongoing transitions to call for just transitions as autonomous engines away from inegalitarian and unecological political economies/ecologies. Finally, I have made the case that it is important to reflect on the intersections of scale and scope as a way to minimize the production of 'blind spots' and 'hidden figures'[23] in the study of emancipatory politics.

In dealing with depth, I have focused on how socially and ecologically egalitarian just transitions are. Central to this is a change in relational power or the fundamental design of the political economy. This may be apparent in considering the financing of just transitions. It is one thing to have a just transition or healthcare or gender equality policy that extends rights to everyone and requires that we craft ways to deliver them fairly and effectively – not an easy task even under the most egalitarian conditions. And it is another thing to argue that existing financial priorities and rules will determine who gets healthcare or whether women should ask for equitable pay or whether only organized workers will benefit from a just transition. It is one thing to decide that we must mitigate emissions and then find the ways in which that will take place and another to argue that it must take place within the comfort zone of business or any other stakeholder. In general, I am sceptical of views that foreground the scarcity of resources as an obstacle to adopting just transition or other welfare policies. This is not because resources are not a challenge, although the data on the sources of emissions clearly point to the impacts of social inequality while military expenditures highlight the impacts of geopolitics. Rather, it is because the first question should be that of the rules or the political economy within which the problem of resources is adjudicated.

---

[21] I am indebted to my partner Mary Van Buren for this general insight, which she employs in her examination of the relations between large and small mining over 500 years of Andean history (see Van Buren 2021).

[22] My thanks to Damian White for pointing this out to me.

[23] My thanks to Cristina Inoue with whom we have often talked about 'hidden figures' in global environmental politics.

I believe I have also made clear my preference for avoiding binary and maximalist approaches. In my view, ambitious policies can take place anywhere from the local to the global scale. Local policies may be more ecosocially egalitarian and ambitious – if crafted intentionally. And global policies can be less ambitious, even though global. I am also sceptical of maximalist views that condition just transition or other social welfare policies on 'not leaving anyone behind' as I think that this often obscures the politics of systemic change.

Given the explicit focus of just transitions on justice and transitions, and the political economy/ecology approach adopted here, I have foregrounded social and ecological (in)equality and (in)justice and, thus, power. It does not escape me that an egalitarian ecosocial society runs against the grain of current realities. Yet, by placing just transitions within the long history of ecosocial politics it is possible to identify massive prefigurative accomplishments, whether in healthcare, education, environment, social security, pensions or unemployment, or with respect to racial, ethnic, gender, labour and other forms of emancipation, despite the serious debates that we may have on how far we have to go (Wright 2013). Historicizing and politicizing just transitions is necessary for the realistic and systematic analysis of what is possible and can help us better employ the formidable insights and findings of the growing and diverse literature on just transitions and transformations.

In closing, I understand from my research that the successes and failures of just transition policies depend on a variety of factors, many not related to justice. However, to recognize this is not the same as saying that power, (in)equality and (in)justice cannot or should not be the measures of just transition policies. Others may choose other criteria and those, as well, will be pregnant with values (Cox 1981; Lohmann 2009; Aradau and Huysmans 2013). Whatever the choice may be, the discussion or debate will be more productive if we make our ontological, axiological, epistemological and methodological assumptions and tools as clear as we can.

References

Abram, Simone, Ed Atkins, Alix Dietzel, Kirsten Jenkins, Lorna Kiamba and Joshua Kirshner (2022). Just Transitions: A Whole Systems Approach to Decarbonization. *Climate Policy*, 22(8), 1033–49.

Adam, Barbara (1998). *Timescapes of Modernity: The Environment and Invisible Hazards*. Routledge.

Adereth, Maya, ed. (2021). *Market Economy, Market Society: Interviews and Essays on the Decline of European Social Democracy*. Phenomenal World Volumes. www.phenomenalworld.org/wp-content/uploads/2021/11/PW-Volumes-001_Social-Democracy_singles.pdf.

Agarwal, Bina (2001). Participatory Exclusions, Community Forestry, and Gender: An Analysis for South Asia and a Conceptual Framework. *World Development*, 29(10), 1623–48.

Alexander, Ruth (2023). *Democracy's Mountain: Longs Peak and the Unfulfilled Promises of America's National Parks*. University of Oklahoma Press.

Anderson, Jeremy (2021a). Part 1: Defend and Transform – Mobilizing Workers in All Sectors for Climate Justice. Monthly Review Online. 2 September. https://mronline.org/2021/09/09/part-1-defend-and-transform-mobilising-workers-in-all-sectors-for-climate-justice/.

Anderson, Jeremy (2021b). Part 2: Just Transition Beyond the Industry Shutdown Scenario. Monthly Review Online. 5 September. https://mronline.org/2021/09/09/part-2-just-transition-beyond-the-industry-shutdown-scenario/.

Anigstein, Cecilia and Gabriela Wyczykier (2019). Union Actors and Socio-environmental Problems. The Trade Union Confederation of the Americas. *Latin American Perspectives*, 46(6), 109–24.

Aradau, Claudia and Jef Huysmans (2013). Critical Methods in International Relations: The Politics of Techniques, Devices and Acts. *European Journal of International Relations*, 20(3), 1–24.

Atteridge, Aaron and Claudia Strambo (2021). *How Can Socioeconomic Transitions Be Better Managed? Lessons from Four Historical Cases of Industrial Transition*. Stockholm Environment Institute.

Auld, Graeme, Stefan Renckens and Benjamin Cashore (2015). Transnational Private Governance between the Logics of Empowerment and Control. *Regulation & Governance*, 9(2), 108–24.

Australian Manufacturers Workers Union (2008). *Making Our Future: Just Transitions for Climate Change Mitigation*. AMWU National Office.

Avelino, Flor (2017). Power in Sustainability Transitions: Analysing Power and (Dis)empowerment in Transformative Change towards Environmental and Social Sustainability. *Journal of Environmental Policy & Governance*, 27(6), 505–20.

Bair, Jennifer (2009). Analyzing Global Economic Organization: Embedded Networks and Global Chains Compared. *Economy and Society*, 37(3), 339–64.

Bairoch, Paul (1993). *Economics and World History: Myths and Paradoxes*. University of Chicago Press.

Bales, Katie, Alan Bogg and Tonia Movitz (2018). 'Voice' and 'Choice' in Modern Working Practices: Problems with the Taylor Review. *Industrial Law Journal*, 47(1), 46–75.

Banerjee, Shrestha (2021). *Defining and Framing Just Transition for India*. India Just Transition Center, Just Transition Working Paper #1. https://iforest .global/wp-content/uploads/2021/11/Working-paper-1.pdf.

Barbier, Edouard (2022). *Economics for A Fragile Planet*. Oxford University Press.

Barca, Stefania (2012). On Working-Class Environmentalism: A Historical and Transnational Overview. *Interface: A Journal for and about Movements*, 4(2), 61–80.

Barca, Stefania and Felipe Milanez (2021). Labouring the Commons: Amazonia's Extractive Reserves and the Legacy of Chico Mendes. In Nora Räthzel, Dimitris Stevis and David Uzzell, eds., *The Palgrave Handbook of Environmental Labour Studies*. Palgrave Macmillan, 319–38.

Barrett, James (2001). *Worker Transition & Global Climate Change*. The Pew Center on Global Climate Change.

Barrett, James, Andrew Hoerner, Steve Bernow and Bill Dougherty (2002). *Clean Energy and Jobs: A Comprehensive Approach to Climate Change and Energy Policy*. Economic Policy Institute and the Center for a Sustainable Economy.

Barrientos, Stefanie, Gary Gereffi and Arianna Rossi (2011). Economic and Social Upgrading in Global Production Networks: A New Paradigm for a Changing World. *International Labour Review*, 150(3/4), 319–40.

Bastos Lima, Mairon (2022). Just Transition towards a Bioeconomy: Four Dimensions in Brazil, India and Indonesia. *Forest Policy and Economics* 136, article 102684 https://doi.org/10.1016/j.forpol.2021.102684.

Bell, Karen (2020). *Working-Class Environmentalism: An Agenda for a Just and Fair Transition to Sustainability*. Springer.

Bennett, David (1999). Prevention and Transition. *New Solutions: A Journal of Environmental and Occupational Health Policy*, 9(3), 317–28.

Bennett, David (2007). Labour and the Environment at the Canadian Labour Congress: The Story of the Convergence. *Just Labour: A Canadian Journal of Work and Society*, 10, 1–7.

Bennett, Nathan, Jessica Blythe, Andrés M. Cisneros-Montemayor, Gerald G. Singh and U. Rashid Sumalia (2019). Just Transformations to Sustainability. *Sustainability*, 11(14), article 3881 https://doi.org/10.3390/su11143881.

Bernstein, Steven (2001). *The Compromise of Liberal Environmentalism*. Columbia University Press.

Betsill, Michele and Dimitris Stevis (2016). The Politics and Dynamics of Energy Transitions: Lessons from Colorado's (USA) New Energy Economy. *Environment and Planning C: Government and Policy*, 34(2), 381–96.

BGA (BlueGreen Alliance) (2021). *America's Energy Transition: A Case Study of the Passage and Implementation of the Country's First Just Transition Bill*. www .bluegreenalliance.org/resources/americas-energy-transition-a-case-study-on-the-passage-and-implementation-of-the-countrys-first-just-transition-bill/.

BGA (2022). *Our Work*. www.bluegreenalliance.org/work/.

Bhambra, Gurminder, Kathryn Medien and Lisa Tilley (2020). Theory for a Global Age: Nativism, Neoliberalism and Beyond. *Current Sociology*, 68(2), 137–48.

Biermann, Frank and Agni Kalfagianni (2020). Planetary Justice: A Research Framework. *Earth System Governance*, 6, article 100049. https://doi.org/10.1016/j.esg.2020.100049.

Bigger, Patrick, Johanna Bozuwa, Mijin Cha, Daniel Aldana Cohen, Billy Fleming, Yonah Freemark, Batul Hassan and Thea Riofrancos (2022). *The Inflation Reduction Act: The Good, the Bad and the Ugly*. Climate and Community Project. www.climateandcommunity.org/inflation-reduction-act.

Blackwater, Bill (2012). The Contradictions of Environmental Keynesianism. *Climate and Capitalism*. https://climateandcapitalism.com/2012/06/14/the-contradictions-of-environmental-keynesianism/.

Block, Fred and Matthew Keller, eds. (2011). *States of Innovation: The U.S. Government's Role in Technology Development*. Routledge.

Bludau, Heidi (2021). Global Health Care Worker Migration. *Oxford Research Encyclopedia of Anthropology*. 23 February. https://oxfordre.com/anthropology/view/10.1093/acrefore/9780190854584.001.0001/acrefore-9780190854584-e-231.

Boillat, Sébastien, Jean-David Gerber, Christoph Oberlack, Julie G. Zaehringer, Chinwe Ifejika Speranza and Stephan Rist (2020). Distant Interactions, Power, and Environmental Justice in Protected Area Governance: A Telecoupling Perspective. *Sustainability*, 10(11), article 3954. https://doi.org/10.3390/su10113954.

Boissoneault, Lorraine (2017). Bismarck Tried to End Socialism's Grip – By Offering Government Healthcare. *Smithsonian Magazine*. www.smithsonian mag.com/history/bismarck-tried-end-socialisms-grip-offering-government-healthcare-180964064/.

Bond, Patrick (2008). Reformist Reforms, Non-reformist Reforms and Global Justice: Activist, NGO and Intellectual Challenges in the World Social Forum. In Judith Blau and Marina Karides, eds., *The World and US Social Forums: A Better World Is Possible and Necessary*. Brill, 155–72.

Bond, Patrick (2019). Fighting Fossil Fuel in South Africa, Campaigners Invoke the Spectre of Climate Chaos. Toxic News. August 29. https://toxic news.org/2019/08/29/fighting-fossil-fuels-in-south-africa-campaigners-invoke-the-spectre-of-climate-chaos/.

Bottazzi, Patrick (2019). Work and Social-Ecological Transitions: A Critical Review of Five Contrasting Approaches. *Sustainability*, 11(14), article 3852. https://doi.org/10.3390/su11143852.

Brand, Ulrich and Wissen, Markus (2021). *The Imperial Mode of Living: Every Day Life and the Ecological Crisis of Capitalism*. Verso Press.

Bridge, Gavin, Stefan Bouzarovski, Michael Bradshaw and Nick Eyre (2013). Geographies of Energy Transition: Space, Place and the Low-Carbon Economy. *Energy Policy*, 53, 331–40.

Brown, Grace and Binnu Jeyankumar (2022). *Supporting Workers and Communities in a Coal Phase-Out*. Pembina Institute.

Bukharin, Nikolai (1973[1915]). *Imperialism and World Economy*. Monthly Review Press.

Burch, Sarah, Aarti Gupta and Christine Y. A. Inoue et al. (2019). New Directions in Earth System Governance Research. *Earth System Governance*, 1, article 100006. https://doi.org/10.1016/j.esg.2019.100006.

Burgmann, Meredith and Verity Burgmann (1998). *Green Bans, Red Union: Environmental Activism and the New South Wales Builders Labourers' Federation*. University of New South Wales Press.

Burke, Matthew and Jennie Stephens (2018). Political Power and Renewable Energy Futures: A Critical Review. *Energy Research & Social Science*, 35, 78–93.

C40 (2022). *Why a Just Transition Is Essential for Advancing Ambitious City Climate Action?* www.c40knowledgehub.org/s/article/Why-a-just-transi tion-is-essential-for-advancing-ambitious-city-climate-action?language= en_US.

Caldecott, Ben, Oliver Sartor and Thomas Spencer (2017). *Lessons from Previous 'Coal Transitions': High Level Summary for Decision-Makers*. IDDRI and Climate Strategies.

California, Governor's Office (2022). Just Transition. https://opr.ca.gov/economic-development/.

CAN (Climate Action Network) (2018). *G20 Issue Brief: Just Transition.* http://climatenetwork.org/sites/default/files/can_g20_brief_2018_just_transition_1.pdf.

Canada, Government (2022). *Just Transition.* www.rncanengagenrcan.ca/en/collections/just-transition.

CCOO (Comisiones Obreras) (2006). *Labour and the Environment: Some Experiences of Spanish Trade Unions in Environment.* Confederacion Sindical de Comisiones Obreras.

CCOO (2020). *Aspectos Medioambientales en los planes de recuperacion post-covid 19.* CCOO.

Celermajer, Danielle, David Schlosberg, Lauren Rickards, Maker Stewart-Harawira, Mathias Thaler, Petra Tschakert, Blanche Verlie and Christine Winter (2021). Multispecies Justice: Theories, Challenges and a Research Agenda for Environmental Politics. *Environmental Politics*, 30 (1–2), 119–40.

Chancel, Lucas (2021). Climate Change and Global Inequality of Carbon Emissions, 1990–2020. World Inequality Lab. https://wid.world/news-article/climate-change-the-global-inequality-of-carbon-emissions/.

CLC (Canadian Labour Congress) (2000). *Just Transition for Workers During Environmental Change.* Canadian Labour Congress.

Cha, J. Mijin, Manuel Pastor, Madeline Wander, James Sadd and Rachel Morello-Frosch (2019). A Roadmap to an Equitable Low-Carbon Future: Four Pillars for a Just Transition. Climate Equity Network. https://dornsife.usc.edu/assets/sites/242/docs/JUST_TRANSITION_Report_FINAL_12-19.pdf.

Cha, J. Mijin, Dimitris Stevis, Vivian Price, Todd Vachon and Maria Brescia-Weiler (2022). A Green New Deal for All: The Centrality of a Worker and Community-Led Just Transition in the US. *Political Geography*, 95. https://doi.org/10.1016/j.polgeo.2022.102594

Chacartegui, Consuelo J., ed., (2022). *Labour Law and Ecology.* Thomson Reuters and Editorial Arazandi.

Chandler, Alfred (1994). *Scale and Scope: The Dynamics of Industrial Capitalism.* Harvard University Press.

Ciplet, David (2022). Transition Coalitions: Toward a Theory of Transformative Just Transitions. *Environmental Sociology*, 8(3), 315–30.

Ciplet, David and Jill Harrison (2019). Transition Tensions: Mapping Conflicts in Movements for a Just and Sustainable Transition. *Environmental Politics*, 29(3), 435–56.

Clapp, Jennifer and Peter Dauvergne (2011). *Paths to a Green World*. 2nd ed. The MIT Press.

Clarke, Linda and Carla Lipsig-Mummé (2020). Future Conditional: From Just Transition to Radical Transformation? *European Journal of Industrial Relations*, 26(4), 351–66.

Clarke, Linda and Melahat Sahin-Dickmen (2021). Just Green Transitions and Global Labour Organizations. https://yorkspace.library.yorku.ca/xmlui/han dle/10315/39473.

Climate Justice Alliance (2017a). *Our Power Communities: Just Transition Strategies in Place*. https://climatejusticealliance.org/workgroup/our-power/.

Climate Justice Alliance (2017b). *Just Transition: A Framework for Change*. https://climatejusticealliance.org/just-transition/.

Cock, Jacklyn (2011). Contesting a Just Transition to a Low Carbon Economy. *Global Labour Column*, 76. http://column.global-labour-university.org/2011/01/contesting-just-transition-to-low.html.

Cock, Jacklyn (2018) The Climate Crisis and a 'Just Transition' in South Africa: An Eco-Feminist-Socialist Perspective. In Vishwas Satgar, ed., *The Climate Crisis: South African and Global Democratic Eco-Socialist Alternatives*. Wits University Press, 210–30.

Cobb, James and William Stueck, eds. (2005). *Globalization and the American South*. University of Georgia Press.

Cohen-Rosenthal, Edward (1997). Sociotechnical Systems and Unions: Nicety or Necessity? *Human Relations*, 50(5), 585–604.

Cohen-Rosenthal, Edward, Bruce Fabens and Tad McGalliard (1998). Labor and Climate Change: Dilemmas and Solution. *New Solutions: A Journal of Environmental and Occupational Health Policy*, 8(3), 343–63.

Colle, Diana and Samantha Frost, eds. (2010). *New Materialisms: Ontology, Agency and Politics*. Duke University Press.

Colorado, State (2022). The Office of Just Transition. https://cdle.colorado.gov/the-office-of-just-transition.

Commoner, Barry (1972). Labor's Stake in the Environment/The Environment's Stake in Labor. *Jobs and the Environment: Three Papers*. https://calisphere.org/item/ark:/28722/bk0003s9447/

Connelly, Steven (2007). Mapping Sustainable Development as a Contested Concept. *Local Environment*, 12(3), 259–78.

Cooley, Mike (1987). *Architect or Bee?: The Human Price of Technology*. Spokesman Books.

Coolsaet, Brendan, ed. (2020). *Environmental Justice: Key Issues*. Routledge.

Cox, Robert (1981). Social Forces, States and World Orders: Beyond International Relations Theory. *Millennium*, 10(2), 126–55.

Crowley, Kate (1999). Jobs and Environment: The "Double Dividend" of Ecological Modernisation? *International Journal of Social Economics*, 26 (7/8/9), 1013–27.

CUT (Central Unica dos Trabalhadores) (2021). *Just Transition: A Trade Union Proposal to Address the Climate and Social Crisis*. CUT. www.ituccsi.org/ IMG/pdf/220411-_web-booklet-just-transition-cut-eng.pdf.

Davidson, Brendan (2023). Labour on the Leading Edge: A Critical Review of Labour Rights and Standards in Renewable Energy. *Energy Research & Social Science*, 92, article 102928. https://doi.org/10.1016/j.erss.2022.102928

Davies, Thom (2019). Slow Violence and Toxic Geographies: 'Out of Sight' to Whom? *Environment and Planning C: Politics and Space*, 40(2), 409-27.

Delina, Laurence L. and Benjamin K. Sovacool (2018). Of Temporality and Plurality: An Epistemic and Governance Agenda for Accelerating Just Transitions for Energy Access and Sustainable Development. *Current Opinion in Environmental Sustainability*, 34, 1–6.

Dewey, Scott (2019). Working-Class Environmentalism in America. *Oxford Research Encyclopedias: American History*. https://oxfordre.com/american history/abstract/10.1093/acrefore/9780199329175.001.0001/acrefore-9780199329175-e-690?rskey=JRyUtz&result=2.

Dicken, Peter (2015). *Global Shift: Mapping the Changing Contours of the World Economy.*7th ed. Guilford Press.

Doorey, David J. (2017). Just Transitions Law: Putting Labour Law to Work on Climate Change. Journal of Environmental Law and Practice, 30(2), 201–39.

Dos Santos, Theotonio (1969). The Structure of Dependence. *American Economic Review*, 60(2), 231–6.

Dreiling, Michael (1998). From Margin to Center: Environmental Justice and Social Unionism as Sites for Intermovement Solidarity. *Race, Gender & Class*, 6(1), 51–69.

Dryzek, John (2022). *The Politics of the Earth*, 4th ed. Oxford University Press.

Duit, Andreas, Peter Feindt and James Meadowcroft (2016). Greening Leviathan: The Rise of the Environmental State? *Environmental Politics*, 25(1), 1–23.

Eckersley, Robyn (2021). Greening States and Societies. From Transitions to Great Transformations. *Environmental Politics*, 30(1–2), 245–65.

Ehresman, Timothy and Dimitris Stevis (2018). International Environmental and Ecological Justice. In Gabriela Kütting and Kyle Herman, eds., *Global Environmental Politics: Concepts, Theories and Case Studies*, 2nd ed. Routledge, 103–20.

Engleton-Pierce, Matthew and Samuel Knafo (2020). Introduction: The Political Economy of Managerialism. *Review of International Political Economy*, 27(4), 763–79.

Esping-Andersen, Gøsta (1990). *The Three Worlds of Welfare Capitalism.* Polity Press.

Esping-Andersen, Gøsta and John Myles (2014). The Welfare State and Redistribution. In David Grusky, ed., *Social Stratification. Class, Race, and Gender in Sociological Perspective*. 4th ed. Routledge, 52–8.

ETUC (European Trade Union Confederation) (2007). *Climate Change and Employment*. www.etuc.org/en/climate-change-and-employment.

ETUI (European Trade Union Institute) and ETUC (2021). *Towards a New Socio-Ecological Contract*. Conference videos. 3–5 February. www.etui.org/fr/events/towards-new-socio-ecological-contract.

ETUI (2022). *Just Transition beyond Growth Conference*. www.etui.org/events/just-transition-beyond-growth.

European Commission (2019). *A European Green Deal: Striving to be the First Climate-Neutral Continent*. https://ec.europa.eu/info/strategy/priorities-2019-2024/european-green-deal_en.

European Commission (2022). *The Just Transition Mechanism: Making Sure No One Is Left Behind*. European Commission https://ec.europa.eu/info/strategy/priorities-2019-2024/european-green-deal/finance-and-green-deal/just-transition-mechanism/just-transition-funding-sources_en.

Evans, Geoff (2007). A Just Transition from Coal to Renewable Energy in the Hunter Valley of New South Wales, Australia. *International Journal of Environment, Workplace and Employment*, 3(3–4), 175–94.

Evans, Geoff (2009). A Just Transition to Sustainability in a Climate Change Hot Spot: The Hunter Valley, Australia. Dissertation, University of Newcastle, New South Wales.

Evans, Geoff (2010). A Rising Tide: Linking Local and Global Climate Justice. *Journal of Australian Political Economy*, 66, 199–221.

Evans, Geoff and Liam Phelan (2016). Transition to a Post-Carbon Society: Linking Environmental Justice and Just Transition Discourses. *Energy Policy*, 99, 329–39.

Farrell, Caroline (2012). A Just Transition: Lessons Learned from the Environmental Justice Movement. *Duke Forum for Law and Social Change*, (4), 45–63.

Felli, Romain (2014). An Alternative Socio-ecological Strategy? International Trade Unions Engagement with Climate Change. *Review of International Political Economy*, 21(2), 372–98.

Felli, Romain (2021). *The Great Adaptation: Climate, Capitalism and Catastrophe*. Verso.

Ferrer Márquez, Antonio, Begoña María-Tomé Gil and Olga López Maeztu (2019). The Contribution of Social Dialogue to the 2030 Agenda: Promoting a Just Transition Towards Sustainable Economies and Societies for All. International Trade Union Confederation. www.ituc-csi.org/social-dia logue-for-sdgs-promoting-just-transition.

Flanagan, Frances and Caleb Goods (2022). Climate Change and Industrial Relations: Reflections on an Emerging Field. *Journal of Industrial Relations*, 64(4), 479–98.

Frank, Andre Gunder (1966). The Development of Underdevelopment. *Monthly Review*, 18(4), 17–31.

Fraser, Nancy (2017). From Progressive Neoliberalism to Trump – and Beyond, *American Affairs*, 1(4). https://americanaffairsjournal.org/2017/11/progres sive-neoliberalism-trump-beyond/.

Frieden, Jeffry (2020). *Global Capitalism: Its Fall and Rise in the Twentieth Century and Its Stumbles in the Twenty-First*. Norton.

Fossil Fuel Non-Proliferation Treaty (2022). https://fossilfueltreaty.org/.

Galgóczi, Béla (2019). *Towards a Just Transition: Coal, Cars and the World of Work*. European Trade Union Institute.

Galgóczi, Béla and Philippe Pochet (2022) Introduction: Welfare States Confronted by the Challenges of Climate Change: A Short Review of the Issues and Possible Impacts. *Transfer*, 28(3), 307–16.

Gaventa, John (1980). *Power and Powerlessness: Quiessence and Rebellion in an Appalachian Valley*. University of Illinois Press.

Geels, Frank (2014). Regime Resistance against Low-Carbon Transitions: Introducing Politics and Power into the Multi-Level Perspective. *Theory, Culture & Society*, 31(5), 21–40.

Gereluk, Winston and Lucien Royer (2001). *Sustainable Development of the Global Economy: A Trade Union Perspective*. International Labour Office.

Gil, Begoña María-Tomé (2013). Moving towards Eco-Unionism: Reflecting the Spanish Experience. In Nora Räthzel and David Uzzell, eds., *Trade Unions in the Green Economy: Working for the Environment*. Routledge, pp.64–77.

Gismondi, Michael (2019). Historicizing Transitions: The Value of Historical Theory to Energy Transition Research. *Energy Research & Social Science*, 36, 193–8.

Glynn, Peter, Andrzej Błachowicz and Mark Nicholls (2020). *Reflection Paper: Incorporating Just Transition Strategies in Developing Country Nationally*

Determined Contributions. Climate Strategies. https://climatestrategies.org/wp-content/uploads/2020/03/CS_Just-Transition-NDCs-report_web.pdf.

Goddard, George and Megan Farrelly (2018). Just Transition Management: Balancing Just Outcomes with Just Processes in Australian Renewable Energy Transitions. *Applied Energy*, 225, 110–23.

Goods, Caleb (2013). A Just Transition to a Green Economy: Evaluating the Response of Australian Unions. *Australian Bulletin of Labour*, 39(2), 13–33.

Gordon, Robert W. (2004). *Environmental Blues: Working-Class Environmentalism and the Labor-Environmental Alliance, 1968–1985*. Dissertation, Wayne State University.

Gorz, Andre (1968[1967]). Reform and Revolution. In Ralph Miliband and John Saville, eds., *The Socialist Register 1968*. The Merlin Press, 111–43.

Gottlieb, Robert (2005). *Forcing the Spring: The Transformation of the American Environmental Movement*. Rev ed. Island Press.

Gough, Jamie (2010). Workers' Strategies to Secure Jobs, their Uses of Scale, and Competing Economic Moralities: Rethinking the Geography of Justice. *Political Geography*, 29, 130–39.

Gough, Ian (2019). Universal Basic Services: A Theoretical and Moral Framework. *The Political Quarterly*, 90(3), 534–42.

Gould, Anthony, Michael Barry and Adrian Wilkinson (2015). Varieties of Capitalism Revisited: Current Debates and Possible Directions. *Relations Industrielles/Industrial Relations*, 70(4), 587–602.

Gould, Kenneth, Tammy Lewis and J. Timmons Roberts (2004). Blue-green Coalitions: Constraints and Possibilities in the Post 9-11 Political Environment. *Journal of World-Systems Research* 10 (1), 91–116.

Grossman, Richard and Gail Daneker (1979). *Energy, Jobs and the Economy*. Alyson Publications.

Grove, Richard (1994). *Green Imperialism*. Cambridge University Press.

Guerrero, Dorothy (2011). The Global Climate Justice Movement. In Martin Albrow and Kakan Seckinelgin, eds., *Global Civil Society 2011: Globality and the Absence of Justice*. Palgrave Macmillan, 120–6.

Gutler, Konrad, David Low Beer and Jeremias Herberg (2021). Scaling Just Transitions: Legitimation Strategies in Coal Phase-Out Commissions in Canada and Germany. *Political Geography*, 88, article 102406 https://doi.org/10.1016/j.polgeo.2021.102406.

Hadwiger, Felix (2018). *Global Framework Agreements: Achieving Decent Work in Global Supply Chains*. Background paper. ACTRAV, ILO. www.ilo.org/wcmsp5/groups/public/–ed_dialogue/–actrav/documents/publication/wcms_759477.pdf.

Hagmann, Jonas and Thomas Biersteker (2014). Beyond the Published Discipline: Toward a Critical Pedagogy of International Studies. *European Journal of International Relations*, 20(2), 291–315.

Hall, Peter and David Soskice, eds. (2001). *Varieties of Capitalism: The Institutional Foundations of Comparative Advantage*. Oxford University Press.

Hampton, Paul (2015). *Workers and Trade Unions for Climate Solidarity: Tackling Climate Change in a Neoliberal World*. Routledge.

Harrison, Jill (2014). Neoliberal Environmental Justice: Mainstream Ideas of Political Conflict over Agricultural Pesticides in the United States. *Environmental Politics*, 23(4), 650–69.

Harvey, David (1995). Militant Particularism and Global Ambition: The Conceptual Politics of Place, Space and Environment in the Work of Raymond Williams. *Social Text*, 42, 69–98.

Harvey, Samantha (2018). Leave No Worker Behind: Will the Just Transition Movement Survive Mainstream Adoption? *Earth Island Journal*, summer 2018. www.earthisland.org/journal/index.php/magazine/entry/leave_no_worker_behind/.

Healy, Noel and John Barry (2017). Politicizing Energy Justice and Energy System Transitions: Fossil Fuel Divestment and a Just Transition. *Energy Policy*, 108, 451–59.

Heffron, Raphael and Darren McCauley (2018). What Is the Just Transition? *Geoforum*, 88, 74–77.

Heffron, Raphael (2022). *Achieving Just Transition to a Low-Carbon Economy*. Palgrave Macmillan.

Hess, David J. (2014). Sustainability Transitions: A Political Coalition Perspective. *Research Policy*, 43, 278–83.

Hess, David J. (2019). Cooler Coalitions for a Warmer Planet: A Review of Political Strategies for Accelerating Energy Transitions. *Energy Research & Social Science*. 57. https://doi.org/10.1016/j.erss.2019.101246.

Hess, David J., Rachel G. McKane and Kaelee Belletto (2021). Advocating a Just Transition in Appalachia: Civil Society and Industrial Change in a Carbon-Intensive Region. *Energy Research & Social Science*, 75. https://doi.org/10.1016/j.erss.2021.102004.

Hessel, Dieter (2007). *Eco-Justice Ethics: A Brief Overview*. http://ecojustice now.org/resources/Eco-Justice-Ethics/Eco-Justice-Ethics-(Brief-Overview).pdf.

Hickel, Jason and Giorgos Kallis (2019). Is Green Growth Possible? *New Political Economy*, 25(4), 469–86.

Hochstetler, Kathryn (2021). *Political Economy of Energy Transition: Wind and Solar in Brazil and South Africa*. Cambridge University Press.

Hogler, Raymond (2004). *Employment Relations in the United States: Law, Policy, and Practice*. Sage.

Holifield, Ryan, Michael Porter and Gordon Walker (2009). Introduction: Spaces of Environmental Justice: Frameworks for Critical Engagement. *Antipode*, 41(4), 591–612.

Hopwood, Bill, Mary Mellor and Geoff O'Brien (2005). Sustainable Development: Mapping Different Approaches. *Sustainable Development*, 13(1), 38–52.

Houeland, Camilla and David Jordhus-Lier (2022). 'Not My Task': Role Perceptions in a Green Transition among Shop Stewards in the Norwegian Petroleum Industry. *Journal of Industrial Relations*, 64(4), 522–543.

Hughes, Sarah and Matthew Hoffman (2020). Just Urban Transitions: Toward a Research Agenda. *WIREs Climate Change*, 11.

Hultgren, John and Dimitris Stevis (2020). Interrogating Socio-ecological Coalitions: Environmentalist Engagements with Labor and Immigrants' Rights in the United States. *Environmental Politics*, 29(3), 457–78.

ICFTU (International Confederation of Free Trade Unions) (1997). *Climate Change and Jobs: Towards a Strategy for Sustainable Development: Trade Union Statement to the Kyoto Conference (1–10 December 1997)*. ICFTU.

IISD SDG Knowledge Hub (2018). *NGO Brief: Just Transition in Focus* (31 May). http://sdg.iisd.org/commentary/policy-briefs/ngo-brief-just-transition-in-focus/

Illinois, Office of the Governor (2021). *Illinois Takes Bold Climate Action*. www2.illinois.gov/IISNews/23893-Climate_and_Equitable_Jobs_Act.pdf.

International Labour Organization (2015). *Guidelines for a Just Transition Towards Environmentally Sustainable Economies and Societies for All*. ILO. www.ilo.org/wcmsp5/groups/public/–ed_emp/–emp_ent/documents/publication/wcms_432859.pdf.

International Labour Organization, Global Commission on the Future of Work (2019). *Work for a Brighter Future*. ILO.

IndustriALL (2019). *A Just Transition for Workers: A Trade Union Guide*. www.industriall-union.org/sites/default/files/uploads/documents/Just_Transition/a_just_transition_-_english.pdf.

IndustriALL (2021). *Future of Work*. www.industriall-union.org/future-of-work-0.

International Transport Workers' Federation (2022). *A Just Transition for Urban Transport Workers*. www.itfglobal.org/en/reports-publications/just-transition-urban-transport-workers-0.

Ireland, Government (2022). Just Transition Progress Reports. www.gov.ie/en/publication/e0e7e-climate-action-plan-to-tackle-climate-breakdown-just-transition/.

IRENA (International Renewable Energy Agency) (2021). *Renewable Energy and Jobs – Annual Review 2021*. www.irena.org/publications/2021/Oct/Renewable-Energy-and-Jobs-Annual-Review-2021.

Iskander, Natasha and Nicola Lowe (2020). Climate Change and Work: Politics and Power. *Annual Review of Political Science*, 23, 111–31.

ITUC (International Trade Union Confederation) (2009a). *Trade Unions and Climate Change: Equity, Justice & Solidarity in the Fight Against Climate Change*. ITUC. www.ituc-csi.org/IMG/pdf/climat_EN_Final.pdf

ITUC (2009b). *A Just Transition: A Fair Pathway to Protect the Climate*. ITUC. www.ituc-csi.org/IMG/pdf/01-Depliant-Transition5.pdf.

ITUC (2017). *Just Transition – Where Are We Now and What's Next? A Guide to National Policies and International Climate Governance*. www.ituc-csi.org/just-transition-where-are-we-now.

ITUC-Africa (2018). *Developing a Just Transition Framework for Africa: Key Issues Arising*. www.ituc-africa.org/Developing-a-Just-Transition-Framework-for-Africa-Key-Issues-Arising.html.

ITUC-Africa (2021). *ITUC Frontline Campaigns and Four Pillars for Action 2021*. www.ituc-csi.org/img/pdf/ituc_frontlinesandpillarsreport_en_2021.pdf.

Jackson, Patrick Thadeus and Daniel Nexon (1999). Relations before States: Substance, Process and the Study of World Politics. *European Journal of International Relations*, 5(3), 291–332.

Janos, Nik and Corina McKendry, eds. (2021). *Urban Cascadia and the Pursuit of Environmental Justice*. University of Washington Press.

Jenkins, Kirsten, Darren McCauley, Raphael J. Heffron, Hannes R. Stephan and Robert Rehner (2016). Energy Justice: A Conceptual Review. *Energy Research & Social Science*, 11, 174–82.

Jenkins, Kirsten, Benjamin Sovacool and Darren McCauley (2018). Humanizing Sociotechnical Transitions Through Energy Justice: An Ethical Framework for Global Transformative Change. *Energy Policy*, 117, 66–74.

Jenkins, Kirsten, Benjamin Sovacool, Andrzej Błachowicz, Adrián Lauer (2020). Politicizing the Just Transition: Linking Global Climate Policy, Nationally Determined Contributions and Targeted Research Agendas. *Geoforum*, 11, 138–42.

Jordhus-Lier, David, Camilla Houeland and Tale Hammerø Ellingva°g (2021). Alienating Assemblages: Working the Carbonscape in Times of Transformation. *Progress in Human Geography*, 46(2), 319–38.

JTI (Just Transition Initiative) (2022). Just Transition Initiative. https://justtran sitioninitiative.org/.

JTLP (Just Transition Listening Project) (2021). *Workers and Communities in Transition*. www.labor4sustainability.org/jtlp-2021/.

JTRC (Just Transition Research Collaborative) (2018). *Mapping Just Transition(s) to a Low-Carbon World*. Rosa-Luxemburg-Stiftung, University of London Institute in Paris and United Nations Research Institute for Social Development. www.unrisd.org/jtrc-report2018.

Just Transition Centre (2017). *Just Transition: A Report for the OECD*. Just Transition Centre. www.oecd.org/environment/cc/g20-climate/collapsecon tents/Just-Transition-Centre-report-just-transition.pdf.

Just Transition Centre and the B Team (2018). *Just Transition: A Business Guide*. www.ituc-csi.org/IMG/pdf/just_transition_-_a_business_guide.pdf.

Karapin, Roger (2016). *Political Opportunities for Climate Policy: California, New York, and the Federal Government*. Cambridge University Press.

Kaufman, Bruce (2004). *The Global Evolution of Industrial Relations: Events, Ideas and the IRRA*. International Labour Office.

Kazis, Richard and Richard Grossman (1991[1982]). *Fear at Work: Job Blackmail, Labor and the Environment*. Pilgrim Press.

Kemp, Rene (1994). Technology and the Transition to Environmental Sustainability: The Problem of Technological Regime Shifts. *Futures*, 26 (10), 1023–46.

Kenner, Dario (2019). *Carbon Inequality: The Role of the Richest in Climate Change*. Routledge.

Koch, Max and Martin Fritz (2014). Building the Eco-Social State: Do Welfare Regimes Matter? *Journal of Social Policy*, 43(4), 679–703.

Kohler, Jonathan et al. (2019). An Agenda for Sustainability Transitions Research: State of the Art and Future Directions. *Environmental Innovation and Societal Transitions*, 31, 1–32.

Kolinjivadi, Vijay and Ashish Kothari (2020a). No Harm Here is Still Harm There: The Green New Deal and the Global South (I). *Jamhoor* (20 May). www.jamhoor.org/read/2020/5/20/no-harm-here-is-still-harm-there-look ing-at-the-green-new-deal-from-the-global-south.

Kolinjivadi, Vijay and Ashish Kothari (2020b). No Harm Here is Still Harm There: The Green New Deal and the Global South (II), *Jamhoor* (21 May). www.jamhoor.org/read/2020/5/21/no-harm-here-is-still-harm-there-the-green-new-deal-from-the-global-south-ii.

Krause, Dunja, Dimitris Stevis, Katja Hujo and Edouard Morena (2022). Just Transitions for a New Eco-Social Contract: Analysing the Relations Between Welfare Regimes and Transition Pathways. *Transfer*, 28(3), 367–82.

Kukathas, Chandran (2006). The Mirage of Global Justice. *Social Philosophy and Policy*, 23(1), 1–28.

Labor Network for Sustainability & Strategic Practice: Grassroots Policy Project (2016). *Just Transition – Just What Is It? An Analysis of Language, Strategies, and Projects*. www.labor4sustainability.org/wp-content/uploads/2016/07/JustTransitionReport-FINAL.pdf.

Labor Party (1996). *A Call For Economic Justice: The Labor Party's Program*. www.thelaborparty.org/d_program.htm.

Leandro, Beatriz, Patricia Vieira Tropia and Nora Räthzel (2021). Connecting Individual Trajectories and Resistance Movements in Brazil. In Nora Räthzel, Dimitris Stevis and David Uzzell, eds., *The Palgrave Handbook of Environmental Labour Studies*. Palgrave Macmillan, 339–64.

Lechner, Lisa (2016). The Domestic Battle Over the Design of Non-Trade Issues in Preferential Trade Agreements. *Review of International Political Economy*, 23(5), 840-71.

Leopold, Les (2007). *The Man Who Hated Work but Loved Labor: The Life and Times of Tony Mazzocchi*. Chelsea Green Publishing Company.

Leopold, Les (1995). Statement at the International Joint Commissions 1995 Biennial Meeting on Great Lakes Water Quality Our Lakes, Our Health, Our Future. 22–25 September 1995, Duluth, Minnesota, 80–4. https://legacyfiles .ijc.org/publications/C46.pdf.

Lohmann, Larry (2009). Toward a Different Debate in Environmental Accounting: The Cases of Carbon and Cost-Benefit. *Accounting, Organizations and Society*, 34(3–4), 499–534.

London School of Economics, Grantham Research Institute (2022). *Financing a Just Transition*. www.lse.ac.uk/granthaminstitute/financing-a-just-transi tion/.

Long, Stephanie, Ellen Roberts and Julia Dehm (2010). Climate Justice Inside and Outside the UNFCC: The Example of REDD. *The Journal of Australian Political Economy*, 66, 222–46.

Loomis, Erik (2018). The Day in Labor History: May 23, 1950. *Lawyers, Guns and Money*. www.lawyersgunsmoneyblog.com/2018/05/day-labor-history-may-23-1950.

Loomis, Erik (2021). Working-Class Environmentalism: The Case of Northwest Timber Workers. In Nora Räthzel, Dimitris Stevis and David Uzzell, eds., *The Palgrave Handbook of Environmental Labour Studies*. Palgrave Macmillan, 127–48.

Lovins, Amory (1975). *World Energy Strategies: Facts, Issues, and Options.* Friends of the Earth International.

Low, Nicholas and Brendan Gleeson (1998). *Justice, Society and Nature: An Exploration in Political Ecology.* Routledge.

McCauley, Darren and Raphael Heffron (2018). Just Transition: Integrating Climate, Energy and Environmental Justice. *Energy Policy*, 119, 1–7.

Macekura, Stephen (2015). *Of Limits and Growth: The Rise of Global Sustainable Development in the Twentieth Century.* Cambridge University Press.

Malm, Andreas and Rikard Warlenius (2019). The Grand Theft of the Atmosphere: Sketches for a Theory of Climate injustice in the Anthropocene. In Kum-Kum Bhavnani, John Foran, Priya Kurian and Debashish Munshi, eds., *Climate Futures: Re-Imagining Global Climate Justice.* Zed Books, 32–9.

Mandelli, Matteo (2022). Understanding Eco-Social Policies: A Proposed Definition and Typology. *Transfer*, 28(3), 333–48.

Mann, Charles (2011). *1493: Uncovering the World That Columbus Created.* Alfred A. Knopf.

Marchese, David (2022). This Pioneering Economist Says Our Obsession with Growth Must End. *New York Times* (July 17). www.nytimes.com/interactive/2022/07/18/magazine/herman-daly-interview.html.

Marks, Robert (2019). *The Origins of the Modern World.* 4th ed. Rowman and Littlefield.

Martin Murillo, Laura (2013). From Sustainable Development to a Green and Fair Economy: Making the Environment a Trade Union Issue. In Nora Räthzel and David Uzzell, eds., *Trade Unions in the Green Economy: Working for the Environment.* Routledge, 29–40.

Mayer, Frederick and Nicola Phillips (2017). Outsourcing Governance: States and the Politics of a 'Global Value Chain World'. *New Political Economy*, 22 (2), 134–52.

Mazower, Mark (2013). *Governing the World: The History of an Idea – 1815 to the Present.* Penguin Press.

Mazzocchi, Tony (1993). An Answer to the Work-Environment Conflict? *Green Left Weekly*, 114. September 8. www.greenleft.org.au/content/answer-jobs-environment-conflict.

Mazzucato, Mariana (2015). *The Entrepreneurial State: Debunking Public vs Private Sector Myths.* Rev. ed. Public Affairs.

Meadowcroft, James (2011). Engaging with the *Politics* of Sustainability Transitions. *Environmental Innovation and Societal Transitions*, 1, 70–5.

Mertins-Kirkwood, Hadrian (2021). Submission from the CCPA to Natural Resources Canada's Consultation on a People-Centred Just Transition: There Can Be No Just Transition Without a Transition. Canadian Center for Policy Alternatives. https://policyalternatives.ca/publications/reports/submis sion-ccpa-natural-resources-canada%e2%80%99s-consultation-people-centred-just.

Mertins-Kirkwood, Hadrian and Zaee Deshpande (2019). *Who Is Included in a Just Transition? Considering Social Equity in Canada's Shift to a Zero-Carbon Economy.* Canadian Center for Policy Alternatives. www.policyalter natives.ca/publications/reports/who-is-included-just-transition.

Mezzadra, Sandro and Brett Neilson (2012). Between Inclusion and Exclusion: On the Topology of Global Space and Borders. *Theory, Culture & Society*, 29 (4/5), 58–75.

Mickelson, Karin (2019). Common Heritage of Mankind as a Limit to Exploitation of the Global Commons. *European Journal of International Law*, 30(2), 635–63.

Moore, Jason (2019). Capitalocene and Planetary Justice. *Maize*, 6, 49–54.

Morena, Edouard (2016). *The Price of Climate Action: Philanthropic Foundations in the International Climate Debate.* Palgrave.

Morena, Edouard (2018). Securing Workers Rights in the Transition to a Low-Carbon World: The Just Transition Concept and Its Evolution. In Sebastien Duyck, Sebastien Jodoin and Alyssa Johl, eds., *Routledge Handbook of Human Rights and Climate Governance*. Routledge, 292–8.

Morena, Edouard (2022). *Beyond 2%: From Climate Philanthropy to Climate Justice Philanthropy.* UNRISD. https://cdn.unrisd.org/assets/library/reports/report-edge-2022.pdf.

Morena, Edouard, Dunja Krause and Dimitris Stevis, eds. (2020). *Just Transitions: Social Justice in the Shift Towards a Low-Carbon World.* Pluto Press.

Mousu, Nils (2020). Business in Just Transition: The Never-Ending Story of Corporate Sustainability. In Edouard Morena, Dunja Krause and Dimitris Stevis, eds., *Just Transitions: Social Justice in the Shift Towards a Low-Carbon World.* Pluto Press, 56–75.

Moyn, Samuel (2019). *Not Enough: Human Rights in an Unequal World.* Harvard University Press.

Mulvaney, Dustin (2013). Opening the Black Box of Solar Energy Technologies: Exploring Tensions Between Innovation and Environmental Justice. *Science and Culture*, 22(2), 230–37.

Mulvaney, Dustin (2014). Are Green Jobs Just Jobs? Cadmium Narratives in the Lifecycle of Photovoltaics. *Geoforum*, 54, 178–86.

Murphy, Craig (1994). *International Organization and Industrial Change.* Polity Press.

Nayyar, Deepak (2016). BRICs, Developing Countries and Global Governance. *Third World Quarterly*, 37(4), 575–91.

Newell, Peter and Dustin Mulvaney (2013). The Political Economy of the Just Transition. *The Geographical Journal*, 179(2), 132–40.

Newell, Peter (2019). Trasformismo or Transformation? The Global Political Economy of Energy Transitions. *Review of International Political Economy*, 26(1), 25–48.

Newell, Peter and Andrew Simms (2021). How Did We Do that? Histories and Political Economies of Rapid and Just Transitions. *New Political Economy*, 26(6), 907–22.

New Zealand, Ministry of Innovation, Business and Employment (2022). *Just Transition.* www.mbie.govt.nz/business-and-employment/economic-devel opment/just-transition/.

Nunez, Jonatan (2021). *Just Transition: Latin American Debates for the Energy Future.* Observatorio Peterolero Sur. https://opsur.org.ar/2020/12/15/just-transition-latin-american-debates-for-the-energy-future/

Nixon, Rob (2011). *Slow Violence and the Environmentalism of the Poor.* Harvard University Press.

OCAW (1991). *Understanding the Conflict between Jobs and the Environment. A Preliminary Discussion of the Superfund for Workers Concept.* Denver: OCAW.

OECD (2022). *The Future of Work.* www.oecd.org/future-of-work/.

Ollman, Bertell (1977). *Alienation: Marx's Conception of Man in Capitalist Society.* 2nd ed. Cambridge University Press.

Ollman, Bertell (2003). *The Dance of the Dialectic. Steps in Marx's Method.* University of Illinois Press.

Ollman, Bertell (2015). Marxism and the Philosophy of Internal Relations; or, How to Replace the Mysterious 'Paradox' with 'Contradictions' that can be Studied and Resolved. *Capital & Class*, 39(1), 7–23.

O'Neill, Onora (2000). Bounded and Cosmopolitan Justice. *Review of International Studies*, 26, 45–60.

Ougaard, Morten (2016). The Reconfiguration of the Transnational Power Block in the Crisis. *European Journal of International Relations*, 22(2), 459–82.

Oxfam (2020). *Confronting Carbon Inequality: Putting Climate Justice at the Heart of the COVID-19 Recovery.* https://webassets.oxfamamerica.org/media/documents/Confronting-Carbon-Inequality.pdf.

Paddock, Richard (2022). Would You Pay $1,000 to See the World's Biggest Lizards? *New York Times.* 21 November. www.nytimes.com/2022/11/21/world/asia/indonesia-tourism-komodo-dragons.html

Pai, Sandeep, Kathryn Harrison and Hisham Zeriffi (2020). *A Systematic Review of the Key Elements of a Just Transition For Fossil Fuel Workers.* Clean Economy Prosperity Series 2020-WP04. Smart Prosperity Institute.

Park, Lisa Sun-Hee and David. J. Pellow (2011). *The Slums of Aspen: Immigrants vs. the Environment in America's Eden.* New York University Press.

Pellow, Naguib David (2018). *What Is Critical Environmental Justice?* John Wiley and Sons.

Pellow, Naguib David and Robert Brulle, eds. (2005). *Power, Justice and the Environment.* The MIT Press.

Perrea, Juan (2011). The Echoes of Slavery: Recognizing the Racist Origins of the Agricultural and Domestic Worker Exclusion of the National Labor Relations Act. *Ohio State Law Journal*, 72(1), 95–138.

Phillips, Nicola (2017). Power and Inequality in the Global Political Economy. *International Affairs*, 93(2), 429–44.

Pichler, Melanie, Martin Schmid and Simone Gingrich (2022). Mechanisms to Exclude Local People from Forests: Shifting Power Relations in Forest Transitions. *Ambio*, 51, 849–62.

Pickering, Jonathan, Thomas Hickmann, Karin Bäckstrand, Agni Kalfagianni, Michael Bloomfield, Ayşem Mert, Hedda Ransan-Cooper and Alex Y. Lo (2022). Democratising Sustainability Transformations: Assessing the Transformative Potential of Democratic Practices in Environmental Governance. *Earth System Governance Journal*, 11. https://doi.org/10.1016/j.esg.2021.100131.

Pinker, Annabel (2020). *Just Transitions: A Comparative Perspective.* The James Hutton Institute & SEFARI Gateway. www.gov.scot/publications/transitions-comparative-perspective/.

Polanyi, Karl (1944). *The Great Transformation: The Political and Economic Origins of Our Times.* Beacon Press.

Pollin, Robert (2018). De-Growth vs a Green New Deal. *New Left Review*, 112, 5–25.

Powers, Laura and Ann Markusen (1999). *A Just Transition? Lessons from Defence Worker Adjustment in the 1990s.* Technical Paper No. 237. The Economic Policy Institute.

Przeworski, Adam (2021). Revolution, Reform and Resignation. *Phenomenal World.* www.phenomenalworld.org/analysis/revolution-reform-resignation/.

Public Health and Labor Institutes (2000). *A Just Transition for Jobs and the Environment. Training Manual*. The Public Health and Labor Institutes.

Pulignano, Valeria and Jeremy Waddington (2019). Management, European Works Councils and Institutional Malleability. *European Journal of Industrial Relations*, 26(1), 5–21.

Purdy, Jedediah (2018). The Long Environmental Justice Movement. *Ecology Law Quarterly*, 44(4), 809–64.

Raskin, Paul, Tariq Banuri, Ilberto Gallopín, Pablo Gutman, Al Hammond, Robert Kates and Rob Swart (2002) *Great Transition: The Promise and Lure of Times Ahead*. Stockholm Environment Institute and Global Scenario Group. https://greattransition.org/documents/Great_Transition.pdf.

Räthzel, Nora and David Uzzell (2012). Mending the Breach Between Labour and Nature: Environmental Engagements of Trade Unions and the North-South Divide. *Interface*, 4(2), 81–100.

Räthzel, Nora and David Uzzell, eds. (2013). *Trade Unions in the Green Economy. Working for the Environment*. Routledge.

Räthzel, Nora and David Uzzell (2019). The Future of Work Defines the Future of Humanity and All Living Species. *International Journal of Labour Research*, 9(1–2), 146–71.

Räthzel, Nora, Dimitris Stevis and David Uzzell, eds. (2018). Labour in the Web of Life. Special issue, *Globalizations* 15(4).

Räthzel, Nora, Dimitris Stevis and David Uzzell, eds. (2021). *The Palgrave Handbook of Environmental Labour Studies*. Palgrave Macmillan.

Räthzel, Nora, David Uzzell, David Elliott (2010). The Lucas Aerospace Experience: Can Unions Become Environmental Innovators? *Soundings*, 46, 76–87.

Raynolds, Laura and Elizabeth Bennett, eds. (2015). *Handbook of Research in Fair Trade*. Edward Elgar.

Rector, Josiah (2014). Environmental Justice at Work: The UAW, the War on Cancer, and the Right to Equal Protection from Toxic Hazards in Postwar America. *Journal of American History*, 101(2), 480–502.

Reitzenstein, Alexander, Jennifer Tollmann, Rebekka Popp, Luca Bergamaschi and Taylor Dimsdale (2018). *A Just Transition For All or Just a Transition?* www.e3g.org/library/a-just-transition-for-all-or-just-a-transition.

Reitzenstein, Alexander, Sabrina Schulz and Felix Heilmann (2020). The Story of Coal on Germany: A Model for Just Transition in Europe? In Edouard Morena, Dunja Krause and Dimitris Stevis, eds., *Just Transitions: Social Justice in the Shift Towards a Low-Carbon World*. Pluto Press, 151–71.

Renner, Michael (2000). *Working for the Environment: A Growing Source of Jobs*. Worldwatch Institute.

Renner, Michael, Sean Sweeney and Jill Kubit. (2008). *Green Jobs: Towards Decent Work in a Sustainable, Low-Carbon World*. Nairobi, UNEP/ILO/IOE/ ITUC. www.ilo.org/wcmsp5/groups/public/@dgreports/@dcomm/docu ments/publication/wcms_098504.pdf.

Robbins, Nick, Vonda Brunsting and David Wood (2018). *Investing in a Just Transition: Why Investors Need to Integrate a Social Dimension into Their Climate Strategies and How They Could Take Action*. Grantham Research Institute.

Robeyns, Ingrid (2019). What, if Anything, Is Wrong with Extreme Wealth? *Journal of Human Development and Capabilities*, 20(3), 251–66.

Robeyns, Ingrid and Morten Fibieger Byskov (2016). The Capability Approach. *Stanford Encyclopedia of Philosophy*. https://plato.stanford.edu/entries/cap ability-approach/.

Rösch, Lilo Bärbel and Daniele Epifanio (2022). Just Transition in 7 Central and Eastern European Countries. www.just-transition.info/wp-content/ uploads/2022/04/2022-04_Just-Transition-in-7-CEECs.pdf.

Rosemberg, Anabella (2010). Building a Just Transition: The Linkages Between Climate Change and Employment. *International Journal of Labour Research*, 2(2), 125–61.

Rosemberg, Anabella (2013). Developing Global Environmental Union Policies through the ITUC. In Nora Räthzel and David Uzzell, eds., *Trade Unions in the Green Economy: Working for the Environment*. Routledge, 15–28.

Rosemberg, Anabella (2020). No Jobs on a Dead Planet: The International Trade Union Movement and Just Transition. In Edouard Morena, Dunja Krause and Dimitris Stevis, eds., *Just Transitions: Social Justice in the Shift Towards a Low-Carbon World*. Pluto Press, 32–55.

Routledge, Paul, Andrew Cumbers and Kate Driscoll Derickson (2018). States of Just Transition: Realising Climate Justice Through and Against the State. *Geoforum*, 88, 78–86.

Ruggie, John (1982). International Regimes, Transactions and Change: Embedded Liberalism in the Postwar Economic Order. *International Organization*, 36(2), 379-415.

Ruggie, John (2018). Multinationals as Global Institution: Power, Authority and Relative Autonomy. *Regulation & Governance*, 12, 317–33.

Sabato, Sebastiano and Bori Fronteddu (2020). *A Socially Just Transition through the European Green Deal?* European Trade Union Institute. www

.etui.org/sites/default/files/2020-09/A%20socially%20just%20transition%20through%20the%20European%20Green%20Deal-2020-web.pdf.

Sacks, Adam (2019). Why the Early German Socialists Opposed the World's First Modern Welfare State? *Jacobin*. https://jacobin.com/2019/12/otto-von-bismarck-germany-social-democratic-party-spd.

Sassen, Saskia (2005). When National Territory is Home to the Global: Old Borders to Novel Borderings. *New Political Economy*, 10(4), 523–41.

Satgar, Vishwas, ed. (2018a). Trade Union Reponses to Climate Change and Just Transition. *South African Labour Bulletin*, 42(3).

Satgar, Vishwas, ed. (2018b). *The Climate Crisis: South African and Global Democratic Eco-Socialist Alternatives*. Wits University Press.

Satgar, Vishwas, Charles Simane, Awande Buthelezi, Jane Cherry and Ferrial Adam (2022). South Africa's Framework for a Just Transition Fails to Recognize Climate Emergency. *Daily Maverick*. 16 August. www.dailymaverick.co.za/article/2022-08-16-framework-for-sas-just-transition-fails-recognise-the-climate-emergency/.

Schaffer, Johann Karlsson (2012). The Boundaries of Transnational Democracy: Alternatives to the All Affected Principle. *Review of International Studies*, 38(2), 321–42.

Schlosberg, David (2007). *Defining Environmental Justice: Theories, Movements and Nature*. Oxford University Press.

Schlosberg, David (2013). Theorising Environmental Justice: The Expanding Sphere of Discourse. *Environmental Politics*, 22(1), 37–55.

Schumacher, Juliane (2021). *Green New Deals*. Rosa Luxemburg Stiftung.

Schwane, Tim (2021). Achieving Just Transitions to Low Carbon Urban-Mobility. *Nature Energy*, 6, 685–7.

Scoones, Ian, Andrew Stirling, Dinesh Abrol, et al. (2020). Transformations to Sustainability: Combining Structural, Systemic and Enabling Approaches. *Current Opinion in Environmental Sustainability*, 42, 65–75.

Scotland, Government (2022). *Just Transition Commission*. www.gov.scot/groups/just-transition-commission/.

Seabrooke, Leonard and Duncan Wigan (2015). How Activists Use Benchmarks: Reformist and Revolutionary Benchmarks for Global Economic Justice. *Review of International Studies*, 45(5), 887–904.

Shackelford, Scott (2009). The Tragedy of the Common Heritage of Mankind. *Stanford Environmental Law Journal*, 27, Stanford Public Law Working Paper No. 1407332, https://ssrn.com/abstract=1407332.

Shamir, Ronen (2010). Capitalism, Governance and Authority: The Case of Corporate Social Responsibility. *Annual Review of Law and Social Science*, 6, 531–53.

Shamir, Ronen (2011). Socially Responsible Private Regulation: World-Culture or World-Capitalism? *Law and Society*, 45(2), 313–36.

Shrader-Frechette, Kristin (2002). *Environmental Justice: Creating Equality, Reclaiming Democracy*. Oxford University Press.

Siegmann, Heinrich (1985). *The Conflicts between Labor and Environmentalism in the Federal Republic of Germany and the United States*. St. Martin's Press.

Sikwebu, Dinga and Woodrajh Aroun (2021). Energy Transitions in the Global South: The Precarious Location of Unions. In Nora Räthzel, Dimitris Stevis and David Uzzell, eds., *The Palgrave Handbook of Environmental Labour Studies*. Palgrave Macmillan, 59–82.

Silverman, Victor (2004). Sustainable Alliances: The Origins of International Labor Environmentalism. International Labor and Working-Class History 66 (Fall): 118–135.

Silverman, Victor (2006). 'Green Unions in a Grey World': Labor Environmentalism and International Institutions. Organizations & Environment. 19(2):191–213.

Slatin, Craig (2009). *Environmental Unions: Labor and the Superfund*. Baywood Publishing Company.

Skocpol, Theda (1995). *Protecting Soldiers and Mothers: The Political Origins of Social Policy in the United States*. Harvard University Press.

Smith, Adrian, Andy Stirling and Frans Berkhout (2005). The Governance of Sustainable Socio-technical Transitions. *Research Policy*, 34, 1491–510.

Smith, Adrian, James Harrison, Liam Campling, Ben Richardson and Mirela Barbu (2020). *Free Trade Agreements and Global Labour Governance: The European Union's Trade-Labour Linkage in a Value Chain World*. Routledge.

Snell, Darryn (2018). Just Transition? Conceptual Challenges Meet Stark Reality in a Transitioning Coal Region in Australia. *Globalisations*, 15(4), 550–64.

Snell, Darryn and Peter Fairbrother (2011). Towards a Theory of Union Environmental Politics: Unions and Climate Action in Australia. *Labor Studies Journal*, 36(1), 83–103.

Snell, Darryn and Peter Fairbrother (2013). Just Transition and Labour Environmentalism in Australia. In Nora Räthzel and David Uzzell, eds., *Trade Unions in the Green Economy: Working for the Environment*. Routledge, 146–61.

Sommer, Jeff (2022). Russia's War Prompts a Pitch for Socially Responsible Military Stocks. *New York Times*. 4 March. www.nytimes.com/2022/03/04/business/military-stocks-russia-ukraine.html.

South Africa, Presidential Climate Commission (2022). *A Framework for a Just Transition in South Africa*. A Presidential Climate Commission Report. www.climatecommission.org.za/just-transition-framework.

Spain, Government (2018). *Plan for Coal*. www.industriall-union.org/spanish-coal-unions-win-landmark-just-transition-deal.

Stephen, Matthew (2014). Rising Powers, Global Capitalism and Liberal Global Governance: A Historical Materialist Account of the BRICs Challenge. *European Journal of International Relations*, 20(4), 912–38.

Stevis, Dimitris (2000). Whose Ecological Justice? *Strategies: Journal of Theory, Culture and Politics*, 13(1), 63–76.

Stevis, Dimitris (2002) Agents, Subjects, Objects or Phantoms? Labor, the Environmental and Liberal Institutionalization. In Ronaldo Munck and Barry Gills (Eds.) Globalization and Democracy, special issue of *The Annals of the American Academy of Political and Social Science*, 581, 91–105.

Stevis, Dimitris (2010a). *International Framework Agreements and Global Social Dialogue: Parameters and Prospects*. International Labour Office, Employment Sector, Employment Working Paper No. 47.

Stevis, Dimitris (2010b). International Relations and the Study of Global Environmental Politics. In Bob Denemark, ed., *The International Studies Encyclopaedia*, vol. 7. Wiley-Blackwell, 4476–507.

Stevis, Dimitris (2020). Global Union Organizations, 1889–2019: The Weight of History and the Challenges of the Present. In Stefano Bellucci and Holger Weiss, eds., *The Internationalization of the Labour Question*. Palgrave, 23–49.

Stevis, Dimitris (2021a). The Globalization of Just Transition in the World of Labour: The Politics of Scale and Scope. *Tempo Social*, 33(2), 57–77.

Stevis, Dimitris (2021b). Back to Paris: Prospects for a Green New Deal and Just Transition in the US. In Vicente Palacio, ed., *2021 Report: Trends that Matter for Europe: The Biden-Harris Administration: A New Political Cycle*. Fundacion Alternativas, 87–122.

Stevis, Dimitris (2021c). Embedding Just Transition in the USA: The Long Ambivalence. In Nora Räthzel, Dimitris Stevis and David Uzzell, eds., *The Palgrave Handbook of Environmental Labour Studies*. Palgrave Macmillan, 591–620.

Stevis, Dimitris (2022). The Promise and Perils of Biden's Climate Policy. *ETUI Green New Deal*. 15 September [invited]. www.etui.org/news/promise-and-perils-bidens-climate-policy.

Stevis, Dimitris and Valerie Assetto (2001). Conclusion: History and Purpose in the International Political Economy of the Environment. In Dimitris Stevis and Valerie Assetto, eds., *The International Political Economy of the Environment: Critical Perspectives*. Lynne Rienner Publishers, 239–55.

Stevis, Dimitris and Terry Boswell (2008). *Globalization and Labor: Democratizing Global Governance*. Rowman and Littlefield.

Stevis, Dimitris and Romain Felli (2015). Global Labour Unions and Just Transitions to a Green Economy, *International Environmental Agreements: Politics, Law and Economics*, 15(1), 29–43.

Stevis, Dimitris and Romain Felli (2016). Green Transitions, Just Transitions? Broadening and Deepening Justice, *Kurswechsel*, 3, 35–45.

Stevis, Dimitris, and Romain Felli (2020). Planetary Just Transitions? How Inclusive and How Just? *Earth System Governance Journal*, 6, article 100065.https://doi.org/10.1016/j.esg.2020.100065

Stevis, Dimitris, Edouard Morena and Dunja Krause (2020). Introduction: The Genealogy and Contemporary Politics of Just Transitions. In Edouard Morena, Dunja Krause and Dimitris Stevis, eds., *Just Transitions: Social Justice in the Shift Towards a Low-Carbon World*. Pluto Press, 1–31.

Stevis, Dimitris, Dunja Krause and Edouard Morena (2021). Towards a Just Transition from All: Lessons from the Pandemic. *International Journal of Labour Research*, 10(1–2), 52–64.

Stone, Lucy and Catherine Cameron (2018). *Lessons for a Successful Transition to a Low-Carbon Economy: A Report by Agulhas under a Grant from the Children's Investment Fund Foundation*. Agulhas. https://agulhas.co.uk/app/uploads/2018/06/CIFF-Transition-Review-FINAL-1.pdf.

Sustainlabour and United National Environmental Programme (2008). *Climate Change, its Consequences on Employment and Trade Union Action: A Training Manual for Workers and Trade Unions*. UNEP.

Sweeney, Sean and John Treat (2018). *Trade Unions and Just Transition. The Search for a Transformative Politics*. TUED working paper no. 11. Trade Unions for Energy Democracy. http://unionsforenergydemocracy.org/inside-the-just-transition-debate-new-tued-working-paper-examines-union-approaches/.

Swilling, Mark and Eve Annecke (2012). *Just Transitions: Explorations of Sustainability in an Unfair World*. UCT Press.

Tapia, Maite, Christian Ibsen and Thomas Kochan (2015). Mapping the Frontier of Theory in Industrial Relations: The Contested Role of Worker Representation. *Socioeconomic Review*, 13(1), 157–84.

Temper, Leah, Mariana Walter, Iokiñe Rodriguez, Ashish Kothari and Ethemcan Turhan (2018). A Perspective on Radical Transformations to Sustainability: resistances, Movements and Alternatives. *Sustainability Science*, 13, 747–64.

Thomas, Adrien (2021). Framing the Just Transition: How International Trade Unions Engage with UN Climate Negotiations. *Global Environmental Change*, 70, https://doi.org/10.1016/j.gloenvcha.2021.102347.

The Lofoten Declaration (2017). www.lofotendeclaration.org.

Tienhaara, Kyla (2014). Varieties of Green Capitalism: Economy and Environment in the Wake of the Global Financial Crisis. *Environmental Politics*, 23(2), 187–204.

Tienhaara, Kyla (2018). *Green Keynesianism and the Global Financial Crisis*. Routledge.

Tokar, Brian (2018). On the Evolution and Continuing Development of the Climate Justice Movement. In Tahseen Jafry, Michael Mikulewicz and Karin Helwig, eds., *The Routledge Handbook of Climate Justice*. Routledge, 13–25.

Transnational Institute (2019). *Multistakeholderism: A Critical Look*. www.tni .org/en/publication/multistakeholderism-a-critical-look.

Trist, Eric and Hugh Murray, eds. (1993). *The Social Engagement of Social Science*, vol. 2, *The Socio-Technical Perspective*. Philadelphia: University of Pennsylvania Press.

Trownsell, Tamara, Amaya Querejazu Escobari, Giorgio Shani, Navnita Chadha Behera, Jarrad Reddekop and Arlene Tickner (2019). Recrafting International Relations through Relationality. *E-International Relations*. www .e-ir.info/2019/01/08/recrafting-international-relations-through-relationality/.

Tschersich, Julia and Christiaan Kok (2022). Deepening Democracy for the Governance toward Just Transitions in Agri-Food Industries. *Environmental Innovation and Societal Transitions*, 43, 358–74.

TUC (Trades Union Congress) (2008). A Green and Fair Future: For a Just Transition to a Low Carbon Economy, *Touchstone Pamphlet No. 3*. Trades Union Congress. www.tuc.org.uk/sites/default/files/documents/greenfuture.pdf.

TUCA (Trade Union Confederation of the Americas) (2020). *Plada: Plataforma de Desarrollo de Las Americas*, 2nd ed. https://csa-csi.org/wp-content/uploads/2020/06/es-plada-actualizada-agosto-2020.pdf.

Turk, Michelle Follette (2018). *A History of Occupational Health and Safety from 1905 to the Present*. University of Nevada Press.

Turnheim, Bruno and Benjamin Sovacool (2020). Forever Stuck in Old Ways? Pluralising Incumbencies in Sustainability Transitions. *Environmental Innovation and Societal Transitions*, 35, 180–84.

UNEP (United Nations Environment Programme) (2007). *Labour and the Environment: A Natural Synergy*. https://wedocs.unep.org/bitstream/handle/ 20.500.11822/7448/-Labour%20and%20the%20Environment_%20A% 20Natural%20Synergy-2007739.pdf?sequence=3&isAllowed=y.

UNFCCC (United Nations Framework Convention on Climate Change) (2015). *Report of the Conference of the Parties on Its Twenty-First Session. Decision 1/CP.21 Adoption of the Paris Agreement*. FCCC/CP/2015/10/Add.1.

Union to Union (2020). *Just Transition in the International Development Cooperation Context*. www.uniontounion.org/report-just-transition-international-development-cooperation-context.

United Mine Workers of America (2021). *Preserving Coal Country*. https://umwa.org/wpcontent/uploads/2021/04/UMWA-Preserving-Coal-Country-2021.pdf.

United Steelworkers Environmental Task Force. 1992 [1990]. Our Children's World: Steelworkers and the Environment. *New Solutions: A Journal of Environmental and Occupational Health Policy*, 2(2), 75–87.

Vachon, Todd (2021). The Green New Deal and Just Transition Frames within the American Labour Movement. In Nora Räthzel, Dimitris Stevis and David Uzzell, eds., *The Palgrave Handbook of Environmental Labour Studies*. Palgrave Macmillan, 105–26.

Vachon, Todd (2023). Clean Air and Good Jobs: U.S. Labor and the Struggle for Climate Justice. Temple University Press.

Van Buren, Mary (2021). Labour and Natural Resource Extraction in Spanish Colonial Contexts. In Lee Panich and Sara Gonzalez, eds., *Routledge Handbook of the Archaelogy of Indigenous-Colonial Interaction in the Americas*. Routledge, 180–94.

Vogel, David (1995). *Trading Up: Consumer and Environmental Regulation in a Global Economy*. Harvard University Press.

Vucetich, John, Dawn Burnham, Ewan A. Macdonald, Jeremy Bruskotter, Silvio Marchini, Alexandra Zimmermann and David W. Macdonald (2018). Just Conservation: What is it and should we Pursue it? *Biological Conservation*, 221, 23–33.

Wang, Claire, Sam Mardell, Jeremy Richardson and Uday Varadarajan (2022). *Ensuring an Inclusive Clean Energy Transition A Two-Part Series on Supporting Coal Workers and Communities*. Rocky Mountain Institute. https://rmi.org/insight/ensuring-an-inclusive-clean-energy-transition/.

Wang, Xinxin and Kevin Lo (2021). Just Transition: A Conceptual Review. *Energy Research & Social Science*, 82. https://doi.org/10.1016/j.erss.2021.102291.

Waever, Ole and Arlene Tickner (2009). Introduction: Geocultural Epistemologies. In Arlene Tickner and Ole Waever, eds., *International Relations Scholarship Around the World*. Routledge, 1–31.

White, Damian (2020). Just Transitions/Design for Transitions: Preliminary Notes on a Design Politics for a Green New Deal. *Capitalism, Nature, Socialism*, 31(2), 20–39.

Wienhues, Anna (2018). Situating the Half-Earth Proposal in Distributive Justice: Conditions for Just Conservation. *Biological Conservation*, 228, 44–51.

Williams, Raymond (1989). *Resources of Hope*. Verso.

Winkler, Harald (2020). Towards a Theory of Just Transition: A Neo-Gramscian Understanding of how to Shift Development Pathways Pathways to Zero Poverty and Zero Carbon. *Energy Research & Social Science*, 70, article 101789.

Winnant, Gabriel (2021). *The Next Shift: The Fall of Industry and the Rise of Health Care in Rust Belt America*. Harvard University Press.

Witt, Michael A., Luiz Ricardo Kabbach de Castro, Kenneth Amaeshi, Sami Mahroum, Dorothee Bohle and Lawrence Saez (2018). Mapping the Business Systems of 61 Major Economies: A Taxonomy and Implications for Varieties of Capitalism and Business Systems Research. *Socioeconomic Review*, 16(1), 5–38.

Woodcock, Leonard (1972). Labor and the Economic Impacts of Environmental Control Requirements. In *Jobs and the Environment: Three Papers*. https://calisphere.org/item/ark:/28722/bk0003s9447/.

World Bank (2018). *Managing Coal Mine Closure: Achieving a Just Transition for All*. www.worldbank.org/en/topic/extractiveindustries/publication/managing-coal-mine-closure.

World Economic Forum (2022). *Preparing for the Future of Work*. www.weforum.org/projects/future-of-work

World Resources Institute (2022). *Just Transition and Equitable Climate Action Resource Center*. www.wri.org/just-transitions

Wright, Erik Olin (2013). Transforming Capitalism through Real Utopias. *American Sociological Review*, 78(1), 1–25.

Wright, Erik Olin (2016). *Two Approaches to Inequality and Their Normative Implications*. https://items.ssrc.org/what-is-inequality/two-approaches-to-inequality-and-their-normative-implications/.

Wykle, Lucinda, Ward Morehouse and David Dembo (1991). *Worker Empowerment in a Changing Economy: Jobs, Military Production and the Environment*. The Apex Press.

Young, Iris Marion (2000). *Inclusion and Democracy*. Oxford University Press.

Young, Iris Marion (2006). Responsibility and Global Justice: A Social Connection Model. *Social Philosophy & Policy*, 23(1), 102–30.

Zabin, Carol, Abigail Martin, Rachel Morello-Frosch, Manuel Pastor and Jim Sadd (2016). *Advancing Equity in California Climate Policy: A New Social Contract for Low-Carbon Transition*. http://laborcenter.berkeley.edu/pdf/2016/Advancing-Equity-Executive-Summary.pdf.

Zografos, Christos and Paul Robbins (2020). Green Sacrifice Zones, or Why a Green New Deal cannot Ignore the Cost Shifts of Just Transitions. *One Earth*, 3(5), 543–46.

Acknowledgements

There are many people who have shaped the ideas travelling through this short book. Here I want to acknowledge my co-authors and collaborators on the topic of just transitions: Nora Räthzel and David Uzzell for taking me along in the foundation of environmental labour studies and more; Romain Felli for reaching out and sharing his work on global unions and just transition with me; Dunja Krause and Edouard Morena for including me in the Just Transition Research Collaborative; J. Mijin Cha, Vivian Price and Todd Vachon for being my collaborators in the Just Transition Listening Project Research Group; and Stefania Barca, Rocío Hiraldo and Dunja Krause for being my collaborators in The Just Transition and Care Initiative.

I am thankful to Jeremy Anderson, Bruno Dobrusin, Woody Aroun and the two anonymous reviewers. They were individually and collectively the most constructive and inspiring set of readers. Thank you to the editors Aarti Gupta amd Frank Biermann for inviting me and for their graceful patience.

I dedicate this Element to Mary Van Buren, my partner in life. Her unblinking quest for understanding the impacts of more than 500 years of continental and global imperialism on the people of the Andes, and beyond, has shaped the way I look at the world.

About the Author

Dimitris Stevis is Professor of World Politics and a founder and co-director of the Center for Environmental Justice at Colorado State University. He has co-edited *The Handbook of Environmental Labour Studies* (Palgrave Macmillan, 2021) and *Just Transitions: Social Justice in the Shift Towards a Low-Carbon World* (Pluto Press, 2020).

Cambridge Elements ☰

Earth System Governance

Frank Biermann
Utrecht University

Frank Biermann is Research Professor of Global Sustainability Governance with the Copernicus Institute of Sustainable Development, Utrecht University, the Netherlands. He is the founding Chair of the Earth System Governance Project, a global transdisciplinary research network launched in 2009; and Editor-in-Chief of the new peer-reviewed journal *Earth System Governance* (Elsevier). In April 2018, he won a European Research Council Advanced Grant for a research program on the steering effects of the Sustainable Development Goals.

Aarti Gupta
Wageningen University

Aarti Gupta is Professor of Global Environmental Governance at Wageningen University, The Netherlands. She is Lead Faculty and a member of the Scientific Steering Committee of the Earth System Governance (ESG) Project and a Coordinating Lead Author of its 2018 Science and Implementation Plan. She is also principal investigator of the Dutch Research Council-funded TRANSGOV project on the Transformative Potential of Transparency in Climate Governance. She holds a PhD from Yale University in environmental studies.

Michael Mason
London School of Economics and Political Science (LSE)

Michael Mason is Associate Professor in the Department of Geography and Environment at the London School of Economics and Political Science (LSE). At LSE he is also Director of the Middle East Centre and an Associate of the Grantham Institute on Climate Change and the Environment. Alongside his academic research on environmental politics and governance, he has advised various governments and international organisations on environmental policy issues, including the European Commission, ICRC, NATO, the UK Government (FCDO), and UNDP.

About the Series

Linked with the Earth System Governance Project, this exciting new series will provide concise but authoritative studies of the governance of complex socio-ecological systems, written by world-leading scholars. Highly interdisciplinary in scope, the series will address governance processes and institutions at all levels of decision-making, from local to global, within a planetary perspective that seeks to align current institutions and governance systems with the fundamental twenty-first century challenges of global environmental change and earth system transformations.

Elements in this series will present cutting-edge scientific research, while also seeking to contribute innovative transformative ideas towards better governance. A key aim of the series is to present policy-relevant research that is of interest to both academics and policy-makers working on earth system governance.

More information about the Earth System Governance Project can be found at: www.earthsystemgovernance.org.

Cambridge Elements ≡

Earth System Governance

Printed in the United States
by Baker & Taylor Publisher Services